Praise for The Meaningful Money Handbook

"Pete has shared more financial wisdom with more people than anyone I know. He is not only a credit to our mighty profession, he's a credit to humanity. He's on a selfless pursuit to assist those who are willing to take ownership of their financial futures. Money is invisible and financial success is about working on future problems. Pete brings these subjects to life and caringly tells you what you need to know and more importantly what you need to do. This book is long overdue; it deserves to be a bestseller."

— Andy Hart, Maven Adviser and host of the Maven Money Podcast

"This is not a book for experts; it is a book for everyone. Pete is a rare breed – an expert who speaks in plain terms."

— Chris Budd, Author of *The Financial Wellbeing Book*
and *The Eternal Business*

"As a marketer, I have a career-long obsession with keeping things simple whether it's a product, process or just the language we use in communications. I don't think the financial services industry is any good at this, which is why many people don't think about their finances. A lack of financial education on the school curriculum adds to the problem. Pete Matthew has written the best simple guide to personal finance I've ever read. Not only will it help people of all ages understand and take control of their finances, I think it deserves to become a text book used in schools to give students a financial foundation for their future."

— Roger Edwards, Marketing Consultant
and host of the Marketing & Finance Podcast

"Pete is a personal finance force to be reckoned with and this is THE book you need to get control of your money. Read this book and learn what really matters about money from one of the best personal finance podcasters on the planet."

— Martin Bamford, Host of Informed Choice Radio

"Pete has been churning out high quality content for years now and he is a financial planner I respect. He is well known for combining wisdom with simplicity and this is a big feature of *The Meaningful Money Handbook*. He has built financial plans for hundreds of his clients and it is great to get that human perspective within this book, which offers more than just theory. This book offers insight and advice for every part of your finances."

— Adam Carolan, Managing Director of Xentum
and Cofounder of NextGen Planners

"I just love Pete's work and Meaningful Money has been simply outstanding in making the complex simple. The tone, language and the delivery style are refreshing and promote engagement every time. Can someone please put Pete in charge of educating our society on money matters!"

— David Ferguson, Founder and CEO of Nucleus Financial Group

"I've been following Pete's work with Meaningful Money since the very first video, into the podcasts and now the book. He has a unique way of explaining all about money and finance that's easy to understand and enjoyable at the same time. The book is a great guide for anyone at any stage of their financial life."

— Richard Allum, Founder of The Paraplanners

"Pete is one of the true good guys in the world of finance. Knowledgable, approachable, with a talent for making money management accessible to the public. His book is the next logical step for Meaningful Money. A practical guide without waffle from a man whose services I have personally recommended. I have no doubt it will improve the lives of those who read it."

— Damien Fahy, Founder of MoneytotheMasses.com

"A beautifully written book explaining complex financial matters in such a simple way, very down to earth just like Pete Matthew. I love the language Pete uses, everything you need to know and everything you need to do. It says it on the tin, there is nothing fancy, just common sense uncomplicated guidance. A great read."

— Lynn James aka Mrs Mummypenny, Personal Finance Blogger

The Meaningful
Money Handbook

The Meaningful Money Handbook

Everything you need to KNOW
and everything you need to DO
to secure your financial future

Pete B. Matthew CFP APFS

Hh

Hh Harriman House

HARRIMAN HOUSE LTD
18 College Street
Petersfield
Hampshire
GU31 4AD
GREAT BRITAIN
Tel: +44 (0)1730 233870
Email: enquiries@harriman-house.com
Website: www.harriman-house.com

First published in Great Britain in 2018
Copyright © Pete Matthew

Paperbook ISBN: 978-0-85719-651-4
eBook ISBN: 978-0-85719-652-1

British Library Cataloguing in Publication Data
A CIP catalogue record for this book can be obtained from the British Library.

To Joanne, Ellie and Kate

Thank you for giving me the space to create and sustain the MeaningfulMoney project for all these years. Your unwavering support means the world to me; it's my oxygen. Without your love and encouragement, I'd be nothing.

I love you with all my heart; this is all for you.

Soli Deo Gloria

Every owner of a physical copy of this edition of

The Meaningful Money Handbook

can download the eBook for free direct from us at Harriman House,
in a format that can be read on any eReader, tablet or smartphone.

Simply head to:

ebooks.harriman-house.com/meaningfulmoney

to get your free eBook now.

Contents

About the author

Pete Matthew is a happy and content husband and father of two teenage daughters, plus one canine daughter, a Jack Russell called Maisy. He plays piano and drums, and has recently taken up ballroom dancing lessons. He's also a super-nerd, who likes nothing more than unboxing the latest piece of tech 'guaranteed' to make his life that little bit easier.

He is a Chartered and Certified Financial Planner and Managing Director of Jacksons Wealth Management in Penzance, Cornwall. Jacksons has been serving the financial planning needs of local families and businesses since 1923, surely making it one of the longest-established private financial advice companies in the UK.

In 2009, after reading a book called *Crush It* by Gary Vaynerchuk, Pete decided he wanted to take the message of simple financial planning to a wider audience. He began recording short videos in the Cornish countryside, answering questions such as 'What is a pension?', 'What is an ISA?' and 'Why would you have one over the other?'

The videos gained some traction, but after creating over 300 of them, Pete switched to the emerging medium of podcasting in 2012, and that's when things went a bit crazy.

The MeaningfulMoney Podcast has now been downloaded well over 1.5 million times, with over 265 weekly episodes in the can. He receives emails from listeners every day reporting how they have transformed their financial lives using the tools that Pete has provided via MeaningfulMoney.

Eight years on, the project continues to be a labour of love, and this book is an extension of that project.

Acknowledgements

Massive thanks to my co-directors Roger, Chas and Mike, and all the team at Jacksons Wealth Management for tip-toeing round the office whenever I'm recording, and for holding the fort whenever MeaningfulMoney business takes over. I'm privileged to lead an outstanding team of people, who make my job very easy.

I'm so grateful to Tom, Justin, George and all the team at Seven Investment Management who have sponsored MeaningfulMoney since video number 100 in March 2011. Their financial support and encouragement over the years have been absolutely invaluable. I wouldn't want to have done this without them.

Chris, Andy and Julie are my mastermind buddies. They (and past members Paul and Richard) keep me on my toes every other Monday when we meet. They are all business owners at the top of their game, yet remain humble, teachable and super-supportive. They have pushed me to get this book done, and in countless other ways too – thanks guys, you're amazing!

Thank you to Craig Pearce and the team at Harriman House, for helping me to fulfil a life's ambition to publish a book.

To everyone who has listened to a podcast, watched a video, left an iTunes review or sent me an email – thank you so much. You give me so much material, I'll never run out of things to say!

Finally, to Dad, Mum, Jonny & Karen and Rachel; and to my in-law family, Terry, Jennifer, Paul & Leanne, plus all the nieces and nephews – thanks for being the best family in the world.

–

Foreword by Justin Urquhart Stewart

IN *THE LIFE OF BRIAN*, it was Reg (aka John Cleese) who asked: "All right, but apart from the sanitation, the medicine, education, wine, public order, irrigation, roads, a fresh water system, and public health, what have the Romans ever done for us?"

Forgive me if you have not seen this film, but it does set out for me possibly the greatest shortcoming in all our personal knowledge and understanding – money and how on earth do we manage our own financial futures. Most of us have gone through a reasonably broad, and sometimes even rigorous, education system. We were told that this was, of course, to prepare us for our careers – really!

Back then to 'brother' Reg. What the Romans hadn't done, and our educational system hasn't either, was to provide any credible or even practical form of financial education. Instead, we are given the three 'R's, only one of which actually begins with R! Hardly the most promising of starts.

For financial education, it would appear that this is covered by a general economics course, which I, for one, would regard as a backward step rather than a creative one. After all, was it not our own Queen who asked the question of the London School of Economics as to whether any of them had been able to forecast the greatest financial crash that any of us had endured? The answer of course was none. Although many commentators have been able to adjust their previous commentaries in an attempt to rewrite history.

The truth is that not only did very few anticipate such disaster. But even fewer had any clear direction and advice, not just for investors, but also not for the greater population, as to what we should all be doing.

Against this frankly awful backdrop of financial ignorance, we must also highlight the actions of certain financially-illiterate politicians who keep changing the rules about investments, pensions, savings and taxes. The outcome of all these changes has been, at the very least embarrassing, but also fundamentally irresponsible.

Enter then someone with some clear common sense, practical understanding and an astonishing ability to communicate. We might just have found a way of transforming a monetary muddle into some firm financial foundations.

Pete Matthew has been a brilliant examplar of what we all need to know, understand and practice. His approach to personal and family financial planning (not so much family planning – he leaves that for others) is really some sound principles of common sense.

Sometimes it would appear that the financial services industry had been designed for the benefit of the industry itself and not its clients.

Pete addresses the issues the other way around – from the client's perspective. Whether they are a single person or a multi-generational family, many of us will be affected in some form or another by all the modern twists and variations of partnerships, divorces and various offspring that come with life.

By understanding what our individual issues and needs are likely to be, then you can start to assemble the financial bricks that can be used to build a financial plan that can fulfill all our future concerns and needs. Common sense? Yes of course. And a world away from the product pushing we see around us everyday.

Pete looks to show how we can secure our futures – not by trying to find a clever tax weaze, which all too often fail (e.g. some of the recent film financing fiascos). He is also not trying to train us all to be an investment guru like Warren Buffett. No, his approach is to focus on our future needs, many we ourselves cannot yet fully quantify, but for which we can prepare, and make sure that we can all have that key word for all our financial futures – confidence.

There is a rather old corny line that applies to this: "If you are planning to invest, don't; invest in planning." Yes, it's a truism, but frankly in any business the same would apply. And, regarding your family finances in a similar way gives us all a completely different perspective from what we normally glean from the media. They only seem to try to provide us with the fear of financial failure or the lure of a fantastical get-rich-quick scheme.

Meanwhile, Pete takes the reader through the process of financial control and planning, but in a manner that is not just understandable. It is also actually entertaining. In his view, money is too important to be dull.

I have had the privilege of knowing Pete for quite a few years now and have seen the practical outcomes of his approach and knowledge. And I can honestly say that it is through his communications, both in writing and video blogs, that he has changed the approach and actions that people have taken with their hard-earned finances.

This subject is vital for us all, and too important to be left to a less than perfect industry. Or either to the opinionated, but frequently inexperienced and (dare I say) irresponsible politicians.

He sees this as a subject that is greater than just you and I as individuals, and also more than just our close family. Instead, in effect, the topic will be vital for everyone in our ageing society over the next few decades – not for tomorrow, but for those days after tomorrow too.

This is essential reading and understanding for us all. Thank you, Pete, for a cracking good book and a really good read.

Justin Urquhart Stewart
Co-founder of Seven Investment Management
August 2018

Important information: The information contained in this document does not constitute investment advice and if you are in any doubt about the suitability of the investment or service, you should consult a professional financial adviser. The value of investments, and the income from them, can fall as well as rise and you may not get back the full amount invested. Seven Investment Management LLP is authorised and regulated by the Financial Conduct Authority and by the Jersey Financial Services Commission. Member of the London Stock Exchange. Registered office: 55 Bishopsgate, London EC2N 3AS. Registered in England and Wales No. OC378740.

Prologue

I have always wanted to write a book. My father has written half a dozen, so maybe the need to write is encoded in my DNA. Yet the discipline required firstly to plan and then to sit down and write a book has always seemed like a stretch too far.

But when Harriman House approached me to write the book you're holding now, they helped me to realise that I had in fact been writing the content for the book week by week for the past five years. Each week I produce and release the MeaningfulMoney podcast, which is downloaded by thousands of listeners. Most podcasters plan their shows in bullet points and just riff when behind the microphone, but I type my scripts out long-form – it's just the way I construct my thoughts.

Each show is about half an hour long, which translates to about 3000 words. At the time of writing I have more than 250 shows published, which comes to about 750,000 words in total. If that were a book, it would be 18 inches thick! I bet you're grateful it's not.

In a sense this book was already written, it just needed to be whittled down from the huge lump of words I'd already produced!

With over 600 pieces of content on the MeaningfulMoney website at the time of writing, I get asked by podcast listeners all the time about where they should start. The book you're now holding is the best answer I can give to that question.

I'm pleased with the result, and I have loved the process of producing the book. I hope you get as much enjoyment and inspiration from reading it as I have from producing it.

Preface

Who this book is for

This book is designed for the vast majority of people who work, earn a living, try to save a bit of money each month, or try to pay down their credit card debt. It's for ordinary people, like you and me, who want to build a secure financial future for themselves and their families.

In these pages, you will learn how to get out of debt as quickly as possible, and learn techniques for good financial control, so you can avoid getting into debt again.

You'll discover the importance of insurance for laying down a foundation on which to build a solid financial plan, which isn't washed away by an unexpected disaster.

And finally, you'll learn how to save and invest efficiently so you can work your way towards financial freedom one day.

If you're committed to your own financial future, but not sure how to go about getting there, this book is most definitely for you.

Why this book is necessary

Let's face it, there are plenty of excellent personal finance books already in existence, so why the need for yet another?

Most books about money either try to be exhaustive, covering absolutely everything, or are very focused on one area, for example property investing. Where this book differs is that for the vast majority of ordinary people, it contains **everything you need to know and everything you need to do** to succeed with money.

What do I mean by that?

This book is focused on **only** the things you need to know and do, without muddying the waters with stuff you don't. It contains the steps you need to follow to set yourself on the right financial footing, without getting distracted with the finer points of personal finance that only a fraction of the population will ever need to know.

For example, as I write this, a high-earning couple could save £20,000 per year each into ISAs and up to £40,000 each per year into pensions. That's £120,000 of savings potential into just the two main savings vehicles. Only a very few people will ever be in a position to save more than this each year, so I talk a lot about ISAs and pensions, but not much about the alternative investments that tend to be the preserve of the wealthy.

For most people, if you learn and implement the simple steps in this book consistently over time, you'll never need to do anything else, at least not this side of retirement.

There are also a few other reasons why this book is needed.

We don't teach finance in school

None of us are born knowing how to drive a car. Instead we take lessons, practice our manoeuvres, learn the theory and then pass two tests which allow us to be let loose on the roads.

Likewise, it is ridiculous to expect anyone to have the knowledge and ability to handle money, unless they are taught. And yet personal finance is conspicuously absent from the curriculums of many schools and colleges.

When we leave school, some of us go to university, where for the first time we are expected to handle our own money, including understanding the student finance system.

Eventually we all have to go it alone, flying the family nest and setting up on our own or with a partner. But unless someone teaches us about money, many of us remain unprepared for the financial challenges of adult life.

We live for today, but tomorrow is coming

Attitudes towards life and the future have changed. Previous generations have instinctively understood the need to save for the future, and the dangers of debt. My older clients all tell me that they never bought anything without saving up for it first. Younger clients often buy what they want now, and pay for it later.

It seems to me that people today (and I include myself in this) live more in the now than our predecessors did. I'm all for #YOLO,[1] but most of us will also live a long time, and for many of those years we won't be willing or able to work to earn a living.

This means we need to strike the right balance between living for now and planning for tomorrow, because tomorrow will definitely not look after itself.

---

[1]   For those not completely down with the kids, YOLO means You Only Live Once. Get ready to have younger people laugh at you for trying to be cool when you mention it. But hold your head high; you ARE cool.

The self-serving personal finance industry likes to keep things complex

Personal finance is riddled with strange terms and acronyms, and sometimes one word means three different things. All levels of the financial services industry have benefited from this complexity by creating financial products with names like Venture Capital Trusts, Relevant Life Plans and Permanent Health Insurance, and then charging you to own them.

Complexity means you need to rely on experts, and experts cost money. Thankfully, the internet is democratising personal finance like never before, and simple, effective products presented in easy language are appearing. But there is lots that still needs to be explained, which is why the MeaningfulMoney podcast and this book exist.

Why me?

Finally, you may be wondering what qualifies me to explain this stuff to you. For the past 20 years, I have been advising clients on all aspects of their money. I am a Chartered and Certified Financial Planner, the highest level of qualification here in the UK.

I also love working with and helping people, and I've come to realise that my job as an adviser isn't really about money at all, it is entirely about my clients. To serve them most effectively, I need to understand their desires, hopes and fears, and then help them organise their finances to enable them to navigate their way through life as efficiently as possible.

Ironically, I was awful at managing my own money until I met my wife. When I was a student, I used to close my eyes whenever I went to an ATM, because I had no idea whether it would give me any money or not. I came to my marriage with nothing except two keyboards and a student loan from the days when I believed I was going to be a rock star. By contrast, my new wife had a brand-new car bought with money she had saved over time, and a credit balance in her bank account.

I understand what it is like to struggle to get out of debt, and I know what it is to manage the highest levels of wealth. I have spent the last eight years since launching MeaningfulMoney distilling everything I have learned into two parts: **everything you need to know** and **everything you need to do**. As you will see, that phrase is a recurring theme of this book.

How this book is structured

First up, you'll find the Introduction, with a chapter about the importance of mindset and a second chapter introducing the three practical steps to take control of your finances. Those three steps are the foundation for the rest of the book, which has three main parts:

1. Spend less than you earn.

2. Insure against disaster.

3. Invest wisely.

You'll find that as you go through the book, the content becomes steadily more advanced. But don't be put off by this – by the time you're ready to tackle each step of the journey I will have explained it to you in language you can understand and put into practice.

I've already introduced you to one of my favourite phrases: **everything you need to know** and **everything you need to do**.

Almost all the chapters are structured around these two areas so that you will have the understanding of the principles involved in each step before you then put them into action. Knowledge without action is just theory. Action without thought and planning is rash, and likely to lead to mistakes being made. Arming yourself with understanding before practically applying that knowledge is where the magic happens.

The book is designed to be read front to back, with a logical progression from the basics of budgeting through to practical investing techniques. You can follow it through step-by-step and you'll be in great shape.

You can also dip into the book as needed, refreshing your knowledge in a particular area, perhaps when something comes up that makes you reassess your finances.

The Meaningful Money Handbook is a practical guide to succeeding with money by cutting out the stuff you don't need to know, and refining the stuff you do need to know to make it understandable and actionable.

Are you ready? Good. Let's get going.

Introduction

The Money Mindset

BEFORE WE GET INTO THE practicalities of how to secure your financial future, we need to talk about mindset.

You see, becoming wealthy, however you define that word, takes a while. Or at least it should do. There are plenty of stories of people who become suddenly wealthy – like lottery winners or 18-year-old football superstars drafted to the Premier League – but who then end up bankrupt, depressed and living on benefits because they never learned to handle their wealth in the right way.

Getting rich slowly is the best way, in my not-so-humble opinion. Why? Because if you build wealth deliberately and carefully, you will learn good habits. Those habits, applied consistently, will serve you very well when you might be tempted to take your foot off the gas and let complacency set in. Also, when you have accumulated some wealth, those same habits will help you make good decisions about how to use your money wisely.

Money exerts an incredible power over people, so it's essential, right at the start, to get your head in the right place. With that in mind, for the first time in the book, here are the things you need to know and do to get into the right mindset.

Everything you need to KNOW

1. The world is full of distractions

If you've seen the wonderful Disney/Pixar movie *Up!*, you'll remember Doug the Dog who is constantly distracted, shouting "Squirrel!" mid-sentence.

As you go through life, diligently following the steps I outline in this book, there will be plenty of things that turn your head. For me, it's shiny new gadgets that promise better resolution, higher speed or superior quality. I'm the kind of guy who watches Apple's new product launches live on the internet.

I also know that money spent on such things is money **not** saved for my family's future. I'm not saying that I don't spend money on such things (I'm typing this surrounded by the Apple logo), but I do so having first weighed up whether they are necessary for me to do my job, and hence earn more money than I have spent buying them. I consider these things to be an investment, but that might just be self-justification!

You'll have your own weaknesses and things which distract you – the trick is to be aware of them and be prepared for how to deal with them.

2. Wealth belongs to those who are intentional

You're going to read the word *intentional* a great deal in this book. Nothing worthwhile happens without planning and effort. No Olympic athlete ever fell out of bed and found themselves on the medal podium. No, it takes years of planning, training, nutrition, sweat and tears to get to the top.

Likewise, very few people become wealthy without effort. In the vast majority of cases, my clients over the last 20 years are people who have followed the steps in this book. Many of them have built businesses; others have followed a career which enabled them to save for their future. Very few inherited their wealth or won it on the lottery.

Some of them learned good financial management from their parents or other mentors. Most of them learned as they went along. All of them made good decisions consistently, and all of them had an end in mind, which informed their decisions. In other words, they were intentional about their financial success, and you will need to be too.

Maybe this sounds like bad news. Perhaps you picked up this book hoping for a system which required no effort on your part, but which guaranteed riches. Sorry about that.

The good news is that building wealth is simple, though it isn't easy. Fortunately, there are some ways that you can automate much of the process, and I am going to share those with you. But you can never abdicate your responsibility for the intention behind the process.

3. No one cares more about you, than you

It's up to you. You are solely responsible for your own future wealth. And that's good news, because no one is going to be more focused on the task than you are.

Yes, your family probably cares about you, and you might inherit some money one day. But why leave your financial future up to anyone else? They will have their own priorities and challenges, which will be more important to them than your comfort.

It's time to man-up, or woman-up, and grab your future by the scruff of the neck, because no one else is going to do it for you.

Everything you need to DO

1. Envision your future

This might sound a bit woo-woo and zen, but it can help focus the mind. Write down what your future might look like if you were financially secure.

Note that I didn't say "if you were rich." Being financially secure is about having enough, but not about having limitless resources. I define it as being debt free, having sufficient income and assets to live a comfortable but not extravagant lifestyle, and being able to help out your family when needed.

What about you? What might a financially secure life look like for you? Would it be a bigger house than you have now? Or a better car? What about experiences – would you like more time to travel? If you could wake up anywhere in the world, where would it be? Who would be with you?

As you think about this stuff, notice your emotions. If you owed no money to anyone, how would that make you feel? If you could give generously to family members or to your favourite charities, what would that do for your sense of wellbeing?

Being financially independent is a wonderful thing. While I'm not there myself yet, I have witnessed powerful emotions in my clients when we have done the sums and I have told them that they can afford to retire *now*, not in the five or ten more years that they thought.

2. Resolve to win

Ultimately, you have to decide if you really want all the things you thought about and wrote down just now. And you have to stick to that decision.

As I've said, financial success is a long process, and there will be distractions along the way. You need to understand this, and even knowing that's the case, you need to **decide** that you will continue to move forward towards your financial security, and reach that point *one day*.

You need to retain a laser-focus, continually lifting your head up from the daily grind to view your future, even if it still seems far off. That *one day in the future* perspective will help you make good decisions in the here-and-now.

I'll say it again: this is down to you, and only you. You **can** achieve financial freedom. Countless numbers of people have done so before you, and almost without exception they will have followed the three steps in this book to some degree. You can do it too.

Let's get down to some practicalities.

The Three Steps to Financial Success

PRODUCING A WEEKLY PODCAST HELPS me to refine my thinking. If I'm not going to lose my listeners with boring waffle, I need to keep things pretty tight.

The three steps to financial success didn't come to me in a flash of divine inspiration, but I suddenly became aware that I was repeating myself a great deal when talking to people about money, and these three steps to financial success have since become a recurring theme.

The essence of the three steps is that if you embrace them and implement them repeatedly over time, you are pretty much guaranteed financial success. After all, as we'll see, getting yourself on the right foot is pretty simple. Oh, it's not easy – it takes work. But the mechanics of what you have to do are not rocket science.

I am convinced that most people have no need to see a financial adviser until they are approaching retirement. At that point, the bewildering array of choices facing you make it a very good idea to seek help from a qualified and experienced adviser.

In the decades leading up to that point, people can manage things themselves, because building wealth is not complicated. Really, if folks just apply themselves to the three steps month in, month out – and year in, year out – they would be just fine without professional advice.

What are the three steps? Here you go:

1. Spend less than you earn.

2. Insure against disaster.

3. Invest wisely.

As mentioned above, these three steps are at the heart of the structure of the rest of the book. Let's introduce them one at a time, before moving on to look at them in more detail in the chapters ahead.

1. Spend less than you earn

The absolute fundamental skill that underpins your financial success is your ability to spend less than you earn. This is surprisingly difficult for a great many people, but without this, you've quite literally got nothing.

Now, I understand that for some people, spending less than they earn may be physically impossible, perhaps because they have out-of-control debt with high payments. Or maybe they have lost their job and there aren't any earnings coming in at all. These are special situations which I'll deal with later, but most of us are not in this position, and hopefully never will be.

Most of us have some kind of steady income which we can rely on every month. Sure, it might rise and fall a bit if we're commission-based or work shifts, but even then, we probably have a baseline income we can rely on.

We also have outgoings of course, and most of these will be much the same from one month to the next. The trick is to make one amount less than the other and then make use of the leftover income to protect ourselves against unexpected consequences, and to set ourselves up for the future.

Of course, there are two ways to spend less than you earn: you can spend less or you can earn more. The best way by far is to do both.

2. Insure against disaster

As much as this book will help you get control of your finances, there are lots of things in life that you can't control.

Dying early sucks for many reasons, but among them is the financial impact it may have on those you leave behind. If you have debt, it does not get wiped off when you die, so someone is going to have to pay it back.

Being diagnosed with a nasty illness like cancer, heart disease, or losing your sight will have a huge impact because you will still be around to experience the hardship. Your income may have to stop, but your debts and other outgoings still need to be paid. This will add a boatload of stress to your life, right when you are trying to recover as best you can.

Finally, being unable to work for whatever reason as you get older will mean that sooner or later, your income will stop. Yes, there should be some help from the state benefits system, but chances are you will have got used to living on more than this will provide. Can you imagine losing your home because you can't earn a living due to severe back pain, or chronic fatigue, or debilitating depression? These are not critical illnesses in the true definition of that term, but they will impact your financial life in a big way.

Fortunately, there are ways in which you can mitigate the impact of these events – through insurance, and by having some money behind you in reserve in an emergency fund. I'll be giving you some ideas as to how much insurance you might need, and how much of an emergency fund you should aim for, in order to put some distance between you and the worst life can throw at you.

3. Invest wisely

Those are just two little words, with a massive amount of detail behind them. By far the number one question I get asked is how to get started with investing. Learning to budget and getting out of debt is actually pretty straightforward, as you'll see shortly, but when it comes to putting money away for the future, we are presented with a bewildering array of options, which often means we end up doing nothing.

How much do you invest for the short term, and how much for the long term? Should you use a pension, or an ISA, or both? Once that's decided, which one of the 3000 or so investment funds do you choose, if any? What about buying property? Or gold? Or Bitcoin?

What level of charges is acceptable when investing? What about tax – how do you minimise that? Isn't there money available from the government to help with savings? Actually, what is the difference between saving and investing?

See what I mean? So. Many. Questions.

But again, most people just need to do a few things consistently. I will cut through all of the complexity by giving you simple solutions that will work for you, no matter what your current circumstances. There is power in the principles I cover in this book to change your financial future, and you can achieve fantastic results if you take action on these things.

And that's it

Yep, that's pretty much it. This book doesn't go into the detailed choices you need to make when you get to retirement. I have saved that for a future book. Nor does it discuss complex estate planning using offshore trusts, because people who need those kinds of things are better off seeking professional advice.

But the book DOES give you everything you need to KNOW and everything you need to DO to embed the three steps consistently into your life. Do that, and your future financial success is pretty much guaranteed.

Let's move ahead to Step One – Spend Less than You Earn.

Step 1

Spend Less Than You Earn

SPENDING LESS THAN YOU EARN is the first of our three steps, and is the foundation for everything else. If you get this step right, much of the rest will fall into place for you.

In this section of the book, I firstly cover why you should bother to budget, and the benefits you'll get from learning how to do so.

Then I give you my tried and tested system for spending less than you earn each and every month, including some simple hacks that I use to make the process as painless as possible.

For many of us, debt is an issue that we battle with daily. Wouldn't it be great not to owe anything to anybody? I want to show you a step-by-step method called the *debt snowball*, which will help you clear your debt as quickly and painlessly as possible.

When money is tight, it can seem like everyone else is getting a slice of your money before you get to enjoy any of it. The taxman, your landlord, your electricity provider, mobile phone company and your supermarket all get the benefit of your money – but what about you?

A fundamental principle of good financial management is to pay yourself first. You'll learn what that means in practice, and how to apply it consistently so you get the benefit of your hard-earned money before anyone else.

And finally I help you learn how to deal with the inevitable setbacks that could derail your progress along the way.

This section is really about helping you build good habits. The great thing about habits is that pretty soon they become second nature.

Let's begin.

Chapter 1
Why Bother to Budget?

IF THERE'S ONE WORD WHICH is likely to strike, if not fear, then certainly boredom into people, it's **budget**.

Like so many words in finance it can have several meanings. One is the Chancellor of the Exchequer holding up a red box outside 11 Downing Street on a certain Wednesday each November. Another makes us think of local authority budget cuts – our hospital might have fewer beds or close down altogether.

But the meaning I assign to the word in this book is the setting of a spending plan each month, so that you know where your money is going.

It's fair to say that most people don't bother to budget. They might have a sense of how much money they have left until they next get paid, and they'll eke things out until then, but that's not budgeting.

Budgeting isn't tracking your spending either, though that can be a part of the process.

Budgeting is about telling each pound that comes through your hands where it should go, and how it should be used. In other words, budgeting is forward-looking. It's about deploying your resources in the best way possible, like an army general planning the deployment of troops.

Some pounds will be used to buy electricity, water or internet data. Others will go to paying down debt, some will be used for fun, like hobbies or eating out, and still others will be used to save for your future.

But why should you bother? Why not just wing it and try to save whatever's left at the end of the month?

Simple answer: because unless you plan, there probably won't be anything left at the end of the month.

Control your money or it'll control you

One of the immutable laws of personal finance is that expenditure rises to meet income. In other words, there will never be any money left at the end of the month unless you plan for that to be the case.

You might start the month with good intentions. Perhaps you had a bit more pay last month and there are no big bills on the horizon. Great news – this month you'll be able to save a bit, or pay a bit more off your credit card balance. But unless you do that straightaway, you'll find that the extra money will simply disappear over the course of the month.

Maybe you'll have an extra night out, buy a couple more things from Amazon than you planned, or enjoy a couple of extra skinny lattes. Whichever, the strong likelihood is that the extra money will be gone by the time payday rolls around again.

Money can, however, be forced to do your bidding. You can control it, and you must. If you don't, you will always be just a passive observer, feeling increasingly frustrated as your financial situation never gets any better.

If you grab your money by the scruff of the neck and force it to do what you want, it will serve you very well for the rest of your life.

Having a budget is the first step.

You'll get to know yourself

Successful budgeting requires you to get to know yourself. If you're intentional about being self-aware, it will help you massively in the area of financial control, and also in other areas of your life.

I've yo-yo dieted for years, but am only now beginning to become aware of the triggers which make me want to reach for a Star Bar. It's a very similar response to the desire to press the Buy It Now button on eBay for something I don't need.

I've learned that if I'm feeling tired, upset or overwhelmed, then my defences are down. I try to avoid these states as much as I can, and also to be aware that when I am feeling those things, I'm vulnerable.

When it comes to your budget, you'll learn to watch for similar unhelpful triggers which might end up with you spending money on stuff you don't need. You'll become aware of the best time for you to sit down and create a budget, and whether or not it's smart to have a glass of wine while you do it.

Knowing yourself is always the first step to improving yourself, and that's a goal we all share, right?

Financial control is a mark of adulthood. The problem is, many of us never get taught this stuff at school or at home. We're lucky if we get the birds and the bees talk, but I bet more kids have to endure the awkwardness of that particular conversation, than are taught about managing spending and saving.

So, it's up to you. Fortunately, although you **are** responsible, you're not alone. This book is your starting point in your taking control of your finances.

Summary – why budget?

⇨ In learning to control your money, you will learn valuable self-control.

⇨ Having a budget is about showing your money who's boss. You're in charge; you get to tell your money how it will be spent.

⇨ The work of setting up and sticking to a budget will quickly highlight your own areas of weakness, the things that might tempt you back into bad financial habits.

⇨ Those tendencies, once identified, can be brought into line through the power of budgeting.

Chapter 2
Spend Less than You Earn

SOUNDS SIMPLE, DOESN'T IT? BUT we all know that sometimes getting to the next payday without going overdrawn or dipping into savings is a challenge.

Remember, spending less than you earn is the core skill that underpins all other aspects of your personal finances. Of course, there are two ways to spend less than you earn: you can either spend less, or earn more.

Earning more is certainly possible. You could ask your boss for a pay rise, or you could retrain and enter a different career. There are also lots of ways to earn money online these days. But what if you like your current job, are scared of your boss, or are not very computer-literate?

Spending less is very much in your control. You can do it, and you don't have to rely on anything external like a pay rise or career change to help you – you can start today.

Here's how…

Everything you need to KNOW

1. Budgeting is about looking forward

I spent years keeping careful track of where my money had gone. Each month I would dutifully update my budgeting software, make sure all the transactions were placed in the right categories and pore over the reports. I could tell you to the penny what we had spent on electricity or mobile phones or whatever.

From that I could deduce where we could maybe save some money, but I never took the next step, which was to set out what I would spend on each of the categories over the next month.

I was always looking back, and while that's helpful, it really isn't the point of budgeting.

Budgeting is about being intentional and forward-looking. It's about deciding where you should spend your money in the days and weeks ahead. After all, it's your money, so you should be the one to tell it where to go. I'll get to how you do that, very shortly.

2. You should Budget to Zero

When deciding how much you should spend on what each month, you should make sure that every single pound is accounted for. I call this Budgeting to Zero.

For example, let's say you have £1,200 each month that you need to budget. Once you have assigned amounts to every category, let's say you have £100 unaccounted for. It might be tempting to leave that as wiggle room in case something goes awry during the month.

In my experience, this can lead to woolly planning and execution. Better to be precise and make sure that the leftover £100 is spent more wisely, rather than just left dangling.

Instead, I would add the £100 to your savings category and double-down on making sure you stay within budget on your other items. Or decide that the £100 is going to pay for a nice treat for you. It's always better to be intentional than to build-in an excuse for loose budgeting.

3. Budgeting is best done together

If you're single and only responsible for yourself, then you can skip this little bit. But if you are part of a couple or family where your budgeting decisions impact on other people, I suggest that you do everything possible to work on your budget together.

For some couples this will be easier than for others. In many partnerships there is one person who naturally gravitates towards this stuff, whereas the other one is happy to let them get on with it. But there is something about shared financial goals that brings people together in a tangible way.

As you'll see shortly, budgeting doesn't have to take a load of time, and it doesn't need to be boring. In fact, as you see the benefit of having greater control over your money, you may actually come to enjoy the process!

When Joanne and I got married, she took control over the family finances from day one. This was a good thing, because if it had been left to me, we'd have been on the street in months. Roughly every other week when she had reconciled the bank account and worked out what we needed to spend in the next few days, she would ask me: "Do you want to know how much money we haven't got?" and I would say "Not really!" And that was it – the extent of our budgeting conversation!

I feel ashamed when I think about how I used to abdicate the pressure of dealing with our family finances and leave it all to Jo. Even though she was better at it than me, it would have been so much easier for her if she felt the burden was shared.

In terms of what is best for your own budgeting, it may still be that one partner takes the lead, and does the practical work of budgeting, whereas the other is consulted along the way. That's fine, as long as both partners are aligned in working towards the same goals.

What if you're the one wanting to take control (you're reading this book after all) and your partner wants no part of it? You're going to have to be gentle. Guilt-tripping your partner will only lead to resentment and certainly not to constructive cooperation.

Instead, try to engage them with the benefits of what you're trying to do, a little bit at a time. Remember that we all have a history with money which may not be healthy, and this might be affecting their attitude. Maybe they saw their parents argue about money all the time and they would rather avoid the subject completely than follow their parents' example.

Finally, remember there is no perfect solution, no optimum way of working. You just need to find one which works for you. Even if the extent of your partner's participation is to agree to watch spending in certain areas, but they want nothing to do with sitting down each month and planning, that's better than nothing.

4. Tools make the job easier

We all work best in different ways. My wife loves lists and writes them down analogue-style on bits of paper. I, on the other hand, prefer to use an app called Clear on my iPhone whenever I need to make and tick off a list.

Whichever way you prefer to work, there are some great tools to help you budget in a way which suits you best.

It is important to know the principles of budgeting before you decide which tools to employ. If you're anything like me, it can be easy to waste loads of time trying software and apps, but never actually getting the necessary work done.

Once you understand the process of budgeting, you can look for tools which work well for you. And the good news is that there are more tools than ever before thanks to the internet and new, more open banking standards.

One of my all-time favourite software tools is YNAB, which stands for You Need A Budget. I've been using it for years, and while I don't follow YNAB's proprietary budgeting method, I do use the app for reconciling my bank account and checking spending patterns.

I reckon it's about time we got practical, so let's look at what you need to do to begin budgeting.

Everything you need to DO

If you haven't already, I suggest you download my free budget planner from **meaningfulmoney.tv/budgetplanner**. Maybe print it out and have it in front of you as we work through this section. The digital version will do some maths for you as you go along, which you might find helpful.

But, while I think you'll find the budget planner helpful, it isn't essential, and the practical steps that follow don't assume you have the planner in front of you.

1. Set out your starting position

We begin with your **Starting Position**. The idea here is that as you begin the budgeting process each month, you will have a picture of what you are worth, what your debt position is and what money you have to work with this month.

As you do this month after month, you should also be able to look back and see your position improving, which will motivate you to keep going.

Start by writing down your net income this month. This is the amount you actually receive into your bank account after tax, National Insurance and any other payments that are taken through your payslip, like student loans. If you are self-employed, this is your baseline income or drawings that you take from the business each month to live on.

In your second and subsequent months of budgeting, you should also note at this point any **overspend last month**. For example, if you went £50 over budget last month, you should take that amount off your income so you have £50 less to play with this month. It's a way of making sure you claw back any overspend to get yourself back on track. If this is your first ever month setting a budget, skip this step.

Next, make a list of your outstanding debts. I'm going to cover how to get out of debt in the next chapter, but for now, just list any credit or store card balances, personal loans or overdrafts here. Don't bother to include your mortgage, if you have one, as that's longer-term debt which will probably take many years to pay off. All I want you to write down here are debts you would like to pay off quickly.

Next, if you have money put away for the future, write it down. Break it down into the balances of different accounts you have, including things like Premium Bonds and ISAs, but excluding pensions for now.

When you have finished this process, you will have something that looks like this:

Net income	£1690
Last month overspend	−£50
Net income minus overspend	£1640
OUTSTANDING DEBTS	
Credit card	−£2000
Store card	−£250
Personal loan	−£3000
SAVINGS ACCOUNTS	
Nationwide savings account	£5,000
Premium Bonds	£2,000

2. Set up two bank accounts

This one really deserves its own chapter, because making this simple change made all the difference to me. For some crazy reason, it never occurred to me that it was possible to have more than one bank account.

That might sound strange, because I'm supposed to know what I'm talking about, but in my defence, this was a very long time ago, before I became a financial adviser!

You should set up two bank accounts, or, as you're likely to have one already, you should open another.

One account – your Bills Account – should be for regular, predictable bills that go out every month by direct debit.

The other account – your Spend Account – should be for your day-to-day spending. If you take cash out of an ATM, pay by debit card for a meal out, or do a weekly shop at the supermarket, it should come from this second account.

On a piece of paper, set up two columns labelled **Bills Account** and **Spend Account**. On my budget planner this is done for you.

Divide the Bills Account column into three parts, labelled **Debt Repayments**, **Savings** and **Bills**.

In Chapter 4, I hammer home the point that you should always pay yourself first, either by reducing your debt or by putting aside money into savings. The Bills Account column is designed to help you do this.

Here's how to use the Bills Account column:

Take the net pay you wrote down just now, and put it at the top of your Bills Account column. If you overspent last month, take that off your net pay at the top.

Next, decide how much of your pay you want to save or use to pay off debt and write this down. I'm going to show you in the next chapter how to use this money to pay down your debt quickly, but for now, just identify a total amount.

Then, work out what all your regular direct debits add up to by listing them in the relevant section in this column. Remember these are the bills which are pretty much the same each month, and so chances are you can just carry most of them over from one month to the next.

In this column I have all my utility bills, mortgage payment, council tax, insurances, subscriptions like TV packages and clubs that I belong to. Regular charitable giving should also go here.

Once all this is added up, you should have an amount left over. Whatever you have left, this is the amount which you're now going to budget carefully. Take that amount of money and physically transfer it to your second current account, the Spend Account.

In summary, the steps are as follows:

1. Get paid.

2. Write down all your debt repayments, savings and regular bills and add them all up.

3. Leave that amount in your Bills Account.

4. Shift the rest to your Spend Account.

3. Plan your month

Now that you have set aside enough for all your regular bills, it's time to budget whatever is left in the **Spend Account** column. This is the money you'll use to fill up your car with fuel, to buy food, go out to the movies – all of the day-to-day spending you do throughout the month.

Remember, budgeting is about deciding what to spend **in advance**, and so the first thing you need to do is to pull out your calendar.

Are there any special events you need to plan for in the month ahead? Maybe a friend's birthday party, a trip to the dentist or a service for your car? Look ahead and take a guess at what these will cost.

How many times do you plan to go out to eat, or to socialise? What will each trip out cost? Add it up and write it down.

Are you aware that you need to go clothes shopping? Decide how much you need to spend and note it down.

Have you ever seen the illustration with the jam jar and the rocks of different sizes? Take a jam jar, and some big rocks, medium-size rocks, some gravel and some sand. If you put the gravel and the sand in first, you'll find it difficult to get the medium-size rocks in, let alone the large ones. Whereas, if you start by putting the large rocks into the jar, and then the medium size rocks, you'll find that all the gravel and sand will fill in the spaces between the larger rocks. It'll all go in, but the order of priority is important.

The unusual expenditure items listed above are the big rocks, and you need to get them in the budget first. Then you can fill in around the sides with the amount you're going to spend on food and fuel for the car.

It wouldn't surprise me if, at this point, you have written down amounts for all the big-ish budget items, and you're left with £6.40 to spend on food for the entire month! OK, maybe not quite that dire, but you may be wondering how on earth you're going to be able to do it all.

It's at this point that you need to make some decisions. They may not be easy choices to make. Maybe you have to tell your friends that you can't go out this month, or maybe you'll have to go without that pair of funky little boots you have your eye on.

Maybe in the past you would have justified these things to yourself and bought them anyway. But now it's different. Now you're trying to get control of your money and tell it what you will and won't spend it on.

Often this is the point at which the good intentions bump up against hard reality. Most likely, you can't do everything you want, and so something has to give.

Try not to be disheartened. Instead, remember why you're doing this. You're going to master your money so that, one day in the not too distant future, you will be able to afford these things easily. As personal finance guru Dave Ramsey says, it's time to "live like no one else, so that later, you can live like no one else." Make sacrifices now so that life is easier later on.

Eventually you should find a balance of spending across the month. Remember to budget every last penny. As you get better at budgeting, this step will get easier, I promise.

Well done! Maybe for the first time ever, you have a spending plan. Now you have to execute.

4. Track your spending

Looking at the month ahead, it might feel like there are lots of days stretching out ahead of you. Over that time, there will be plenty of opportunities to fall off the budgeting wagon. The easiest way to prevent that is to keep track of your spending throughout the month.

There are a few ways you can do this. You can keep a notebook with you at all times and write down every penny you spend, or you can flip open the Notes app on your phone and keep notes there. Or there are apps you can use to help you keep track of your spending in each category.

My budgeting app of choice, You Need A Budget, or YNAB, synchronises my budget on my phone, iPad and computer. When I take cash out of an ATM, or pay for something with my debit card, I make a note in the mobile YNAB app, which then updates the budget on all my devices. That way I can easily refer to this at the end of the week or the month to see what I have spent.

How detailed do you need to be? Answer: as detailed as is helpful for you, and no simpler.

I use a few categories to track my spending. These are the areas of spending you assigned your money to at the start of the month. As you go through the month, you want to categorise your transactions so you can see how you're doing in each area.

Don't have so many categories that life gets too complicated and you find yourself struggling to remember whether to note your supermarket shop into food, or general groceries, or part of it into toiletries. I have one category called groceries, which covers everything I consume at home, from food to matches to shoe polish. Keep it simple – you're more likely to keep up to it.

You'll probably also refine your categories as you get better at this. I have certainly done so over the years. Here are my spending categories:

⇨ Groceries

⇨ Eating out

⇨ Toiletries

⇨ Medical/Dental

⇨ Fuel for the car

⇨ Gifts

⇨ Home Maintenance/Repair

⇨ Holiday

⇨ Vet bills

⇨ Clothing/Hairdresser

⇨ Clubs/Societies

⇨ Misc/Other

⇨ Cash Out

Let me pick out a couple of these for explanation.

Firstly, I obviously don't go on holiday every month, so this category might only feature in a couple of months of the year.

Also, vet bills aren't a regular feature, thankfully! But there are times when I know they are coming up and I need to factor them into my spending. You will find that your categories may change a little from month to month. That's OK, be intentional, look ahead and plan accordingly.

Finally, Cash Out. That's a biggie, and can cover a multitude of sins. We all take cash out of the bank to have in our purse or wallet, and we all know how this can quickly slip through our fingers.

If you really want to drill down into your spending patterns, then I suggest that for a period of time you keep track of literally every penny you spend. It can be a real eye-opener! If you're anything like me, you will notice patterns in your thoughtless spending, and small amounts can really add up.

But we're beyond being thoughtless now; we're being intentional. For a few years I would track my cash spending for one month each year, just to make sure I hadn't regressed into too much mindless spending. It's a good practice to keep, at least while you're aiming to master these principles.

5. Weekly review

Once a week, I suggest that you sit down to see how you're doing.

Let's say you have budgeted £200 for the month to spend on groceries. When you do your weekly review at the end of the first week, you find that you have in fact spent £70. As you're one-quarter of the way through the month, you ought to be about one-quarter of the way through your budget, so you should have spent £50 at this point.

You need to take a pragmatic approach to this. Maybe you stocked up a bit in the first week of the month, and therefore your grocery costs for the next three weeks will be a bit lower. That's fine.

The final column of the budget planner is a progress section. Here you can keep a note of whether you are ahead or behind your target of where you should be at this point in the month.

The point of the weekly review is to keep you on track by forcing you to think about your budget **throughout** the month, not just at the start and the end. The idea is that by keeping an eye on things as you go along, you can adjust accordingly when things aren't quite going to plan.

Let's say that halfway through the month you have to spend some money that you weren't expecting. Not a huge amount, but something you haven't budgeted for. The weekly review is the point at which you can take a look at your budget overall and decide what else might have to give, in order to keep your overall spending on track.

Maybe now you have to forgo the meal out, and eat in instead. That's better than dipping into savings unnecessarily, or worse, going overdrawn or paying for things on your credit card. I look more at dealing with setbacks in Chapter 5.

6. Rinse and repeat

And really, that's all there is to budgeting. By making sure all your monthly regular bills are accounted for by the money retained in your Bills Account, all you have to budget is your spending money across a few categories.

This will take less time as you get more experienced. Before long you'll get to the point where it takes you maybe half an hour at the start of the month, and then ten minutes for your weekly review.

It will help you to embed these practices into your life if you can find a regular time which works for you. Maybe a Sunday evening before the working week begins, or another time when you have a clear hour. Again, if you're in a relationship where you are working towards the same goals, try to do this together.

Hopefully, you are now spending less than you earn. Once you have got to this point, you must keep going. Don't be tempted to do this for a short time and then give up. If you persist, before you know it you will have built strong habits that will serve you very well for the rest of your life, as we'll see in the chapters to come.

Chapter 3
Getting Out of Debt

DEBT HAS BEEN A PART of the human condition since, well, forever. It is a necessary part of life for almost all of us, from the poorest to the richest, and if used correctly it can accelerate your wealth-building. But it can also be a trap, and many people find themselves being dragged deeper and deeper into debt with no clue of how to get themselves out.

Our view of debt (and money in general) is very much informed by the lessons we learned from those around us as we grew up.

My parents were born in the early 1940s and, as such, can remember the post-war years of rationing. Borrowing money just wasn't an option for many people then in the way that it is now, and consequently, apart from their mortgage, my parents never carried a lot of debt.

Just one generation later, when I was about to head to university in 1994, I went to my bank to open a student bank account. On the spot, I was given two credit cards, each with a £250 credit limit. I never asked for them; they came with the bank account as a so-called bonus. But I was never taught how they worked or how to use them.

The global financial crisis of 2008 was precipitated by, amongst other things, too much credit being extended to the wrong people. Eventually people began to realise that this was not sustainable and the whole system very nearly collapsed. Only the intervention of governments and central banks stopped us regressing back to the financial dark ages.

For many of us, when we are embarking on the process of getting our money under control, we are starting from a negative position – we already have some debt and we need to do something about it. Therefore we need to understand how debt really works, the difference between good debt and bad debt, and how to keep debt under control.

Let's look at this now.

Everything you need to KNOW

1. Good debt and bad debt

It is important, right at the start, to define the difference between good debt and bad debt. My definition of this is pretty simple:

Good debt generally carries a **low interest rate** and is used to buy things which **increase** in value.

Bad debt involves a **high interest rate** and is used to buy things which **decrease** in value.

Based on these definitions, a mortgage would be a good debt. As a rule, the interest rates on mortgages are linked to the bank base rate, the national interest rate that the Bank of England sets as the benchmark. Usually, mortgage interest rates are within a few percentage points of the bank base rate.

Mortgages are used to buy houses, either to live in or as investments, and property tends to increase in value over time. That isn't always the case though, and property values can be very localised, but we're generalising here. Ask your parents how much they bought their first house for, and you'll see that generally, house prices rise over long periods of time.

And so, a mortgage fulfils our two criteria for good debt – low interest and rising asset prices.

Another form of good debt would be a student loan. In the UK, the student finance system is different from all other kinds of loans, and I'll explore it a little more shortly, but against our two criteria it stacks up as good debt. The interest rates are low and it buys you an education with potentially higher earnings power as a result.

Sure, the value of an education is subjective, and there are plenty of people who don't have a degree earning more than people who do, but you get my point.

Bad debt is the exact opposite of good debt. Take a store card for example. You know the kind of thing – "Get 10% off your order today if you take out our store card, and spread the payments over time." Interest rates can be 29.9%, that's 60 times the Bank of England base rate as I type this. Sometimes rates are even higher. Store cards are often used to buy things like clothes or televisions, which will wear out. High interest, decreasing value – our two criteria for bad debt.

Even worse are payday loans. Next time you see an advert for short-term loans on TV, check the small print at the bottom of the screen. You'll see interest rates of 1200% and sometimes many times that. These are loans designed to help people get to the next payday; they're not being used to buy things that go up in value, but just to help unfortunate people buy food for the next couple of weeks. It's a damning indictment on our society that people are able to get into such dire financial straits that they have to resort to this kind of borrowing.

Bad debt can lead to a vicious cycle of borrowing from one lender to pay off the debt owed to another, and each month having to borrow a little earlier or a little more than the last, because the money runs out more quickly due to the charges payable on the bad debt.

2. Serious debt and what to do about it

Maybe you identified yourself in the last couple of paragraphs. If so, I urge you strongly to seek professional help. Far too many people bury their heads in the sand when it comes to debt, because they can't see a way out. Worse, uncontrollable debt is a contributing factor in people contemplating and committing suicide.[2]

If you feel like your debt is getting out of control, you need to take action now. I suggest you get in touch with a couple of organisations.

Firstly, the Citizen's Advice Bureau (citizensadvice.org.uk) is a great place to start. They can help you quantify your problem and suggest ways to deal with it. They can also put you in touch with organisations who can negotiate with your creditors and help you come to an arrangement with them.

One such organisation for which I have a great deal of respect is Christians Against Poverty (capuk.org). Don't be put off by the religious-sounding name; CAP is a leading debt counselling charity which has helped many thousands of families to break free of serious debt.

Please, please don't believe that you're alone, or that your problem is unique to you. There are plenty of people who have been in the same place, or worse, that you are in now, and who have escaped a life of fear over their debt. It is not an insurmountable problem; there is a way out if you're prepared to work hard and make some serious changes. Anything has to be better than feeling trapped – get help, and fast.

3. A word about student debt

As I write this, my eldest daughter Ellie has just turned 18 and will be going off to university in the next few months. I figured it was about time I really understood how the student finance system worked, and I was surprised that much of what I thought I knew was completely untrue.

---

[2]   According to the 2013 statistics from Samaritans UK: www.samaritans.org/news/one-six-calls-men-are-about-money-worries.

I went on to produce a podcast episode covering the basics of the student loan system,[3] which was very well received and got me quite a few emails in response.

Put very simply, a student can borrow money to cover both their tuition fees and their maintenance. The maintenance loan is means-tested, which means the amount you can borrow depends on the household income of the student's family. In the 2018/19 academic year a student taking out the maximum borrowing will end up with total student debt of about £53,000 over a three-year degree course.

On the face of it, that's a terrifying number, until you understand that student loans are quite different from any other kind of loan in existence.

Firstly, the monthly repayments you make have nothing to do with how much you have borrowed, but rather how much you earn. If you earn over a threshold figure, currently £25,000,[4] you will pay back 9% of everything you earn over that figure.

Second, if your income drops below the threshold, your repayments will stop until your income rises above it again. That means that if you lose your job, take a career break to have children, or have an accident that prevents you from working for a while, you won't have to make the repayments – they will stop automatically.

Next, interest rates are linked to inflation and to your earnings. This means that for many people, the amount of money owed will never increase in real terms and will do so only for higher earners.

Finally, anything you still owe after 30 years is wiped off the slate. Gone. No more. Disappeared.

So you see, the student loan system is more like a graduate tax than a loan. You repay based on your earnings, and for a finite period of time. Many people will never get anywhere near paying all of their student

---

[3]   You can find that episode over at meaningfulmoney.tv/ls5.
[4]   From April 2018.

loan off as they just won't earn enough to do so, and those who do will have earned more anyway.

Yes, there are implications of carrying student loans. When you come to get a mortgage, your net income will be lower due to the student loan repayments, and your borrowing capacity will be lower as a result. The thinking is, of course, that your earnings capacity will be increased for having gained the qualifications and the life experience that comes from attending university. While that's a generalisation, it's true in many cases, and if it doesn't stack up that way for you, then your loan repayments will be low or non-existent.

All these factors are the reasons why I classify student loans as good debt. Yes, I'd rather university education was free like it was for me back in the 1990s, but it isn't. My own kids will at least have the opportunity to go to university to study whatever takes their fancy without being financially crippled as a result. I will be encouraging both my kids to take out the maximum loans available.

4. Debt is not inevitable

The final thing you need to know about debt is that it doesn't have to feature in your life. Our parents and grandparents got on OK without easy credit, and so can you.

Part of our problem these days is that we are bombarded with images that project a certain level of desired lifestyle. You must have this nice car, you really need the latest iPhone and you really should buy a house.

In truth you don't **need** any of those things. You might want them, but you don't need them, and it is quite possible to go through life perfectly happily without them.

Like every aspect of personal finance, debt should be dealt with **intentionally**, and not passively. Don't borrow money to buy a new bigger TV just because your neighbour has one, or just because you think that success is defined as having shiny gadgets. These are stupid reasons to get into debt.

In fact, don't get into debt to buy a TV for any reason – save up the money instead (more on that in the next chapter).

Make each financial decision with careful thought and planning, weighing up the pros and cons of each course of action. If you can be patient to save for large purchases, you'll be making yourself richer in the process, rather than the people you are borrowing from.

Everything you need to DO

1. Establish a starter emergency fund

If you are to get out of debt successfully, you need to apply the budgeting techniques learned in the last chapter rigorously, month in, month out. You need to throw as much money against the debt as you can in order to shift it as quickly as possible.

The problem with debt is that it has a nasty habit of catching you off guard. To prevent that happening, you should try to establish an emergency fund. This is a sum of money, held safely in a bank account which is accessible, but which is reserved for emergencies only.

How do you manage that if you're already struggling to prevent your debt from getting any worse? Well, you're going to have to get creative.

Firstly, you could consider taking on a second job, or doing odd jobs for people to gather some money together. Don't be tempted to spend it; put it away.

Take a look at the stuff around you. Do you need it all? Is there anything that might find a home elsewhere? Collect it all together and sell it on eBay, or go to a local car boot sale.

Next, screw down your budget to eke out every penny you can. It makes no sense to complain about being in debt if you're still ordering expensive takeaways twice a week and you simply must catch the latest movie. Eat super-frugally for a month and see how much you can save. No, it might not be fun, but neither is having the bailiffs calling round. Stack every penny you can find into your emergency fund and leave it there.

How much should you aim to put aside? This is a starter emergency fund and we'll finish it off later after you have paid off your debt. For now, it's a smaller amount we're looking to get together.

If your total outgoings are more than £1500 per month, then I would look to get an emergency fund of £1000 together. If your expenses are less than that, then £500 will probably do. But anything is better than nothing, so don't get too hung up on the numbers.

It is essential that you resist the temptation to dip into this money. It isn't a Christmas fund, or a holiday fund. It's there for true emergencies, like a big car repair bill you weren't expecting, or having to call out an emergency plumber to fix a leak.

Why not take the money you have amassed for your emergency fund and use it to pay down your debt? Well, if the debt is small and can be paid off that quickly, then that makes sense. But most people won't be in a position to pay off their debt with just a couple of months' hard graft.

The reason for putting a starter emergency fund in place is that it puts a buffer between you and the reasons most people get into debt in the first place.

You see, often it is life's unexpected events that cause financial difficulty. And if one of those events happens while you're trying to pay down your debt, then you're likely to get deeper into debt, unless you have an emergency fund to protect you.

If you have to dip into your emergency fund, treat that as a debt to yourself and pay yourself back regularly to top it back up. Don't be disheartened if this happens – it's what the emergency fund is for, and dipping into your own money is way better than increasing your debt.

The second of our three steps to financial success is about insuring against disaster, and having an emergency fund is the first part of that process. By keeping an amount of money to one side as a safety net against the unexpected twists of life, you are protecting yourself from those unexpected events.

And, weirdly, you will find that in being prepared for it, trouble is less likely to find you.

2. Roll the debt snowball

In my years as a financial planner I have seen all kinds of methods to get out of debt, but by far the most effective one I have seen is the *debt snowball*. I must give full credit for this idea to Dave Ramsey (daveramsey.com), who is one of America's most well-known commentators when it comes to personal finance. His daily radio show is syndicated across the US and is available as a podcast worldwide. I also highly recommend his superb book *The Total Money Makeover*, which is where I first heard about the debt snowball.

It works like this.

Firstly, take a piece of paper and make a list of your outstanding debts, excluding your mortgage. Importantly, list them in order of increasing debt size, with the smallest outstanding balance at the top, then the next smallest, and so on. Next to each outstanding balance, list the minimum monthly payment you have to make on that debt.

Now, once you have decided in your budget how much you are going to pay off your debt each month, you should divide it like this:

⇨ Pay the minimum payment on all but the smallest debt.

⇨ Pay as much as you can against the smallest debt.

The table below provides an example.

Let's say that you have identified that you can pay £300 against your debt this month. You'll notice that credit cards A and B and the personal loan have a total minimum payment of £225. That leaves £75 that you can pay off your store card. In three months it'll be gone!

Debt	Balance	Monthly minimum payment
Store Card	£200	£15
Credit Card A	£1,000	£50
Credit Card B	£1,500	£75
Personal Loan	£2,000	£100

Notice there's no column in the table for the interest rate each debt is being charged. Surely it makes sense to pay off the highest-interest loan first? Well, financially that might make sense, but if you're reading this, I'm assuming you're a human being, and we humans like **quick wins**. By paying off the smallest debt first, you get an easy quick win, which will fuel your excitement for getting out of debt fast and help you to keep going.

Once your smallest debt is gone, you can continue paying the minimum payments against the largest debts, and pay the rest of your monthly budget against the next-smallest loan.

Using the numbers above, and assuming you still have £300 per month allocated for debt-reduction, you will pay £75 against credit card B and £100 against the personal loan. That leaves £125 you can pay against credit card A.

Once credit card A has been paid off, you focus your attention on credit card B, and so on. The amount you're paying off the smallest debt each time grows like a snowball because more money becomes available as the smaller debts are cleared.

This process becomes addictive and exciting. As you see your outstanding balances come down each month, you will look for more money in your budget to throw at the debt. You'll wonder about selling one of the kids or a kidney to clear the loans more quickly. If you doubt the effectiveness of this process, tune into Dave Ramsey's radio show and listen to folks who call in and give their debt-free scream – it's inspiring stuff.

You can do this. Of course, it takes work and it takes time, but if you put in place your starter emergency fund first, and then roll the debt snowball to clear your debt efficiently, you will eventually be debt-free.

3. Finish your emergency fund

Once you are debt free, I suggest you add a little bit more money to your emergency fund. You should now have a decent sum of money available in your budget each month, with which you have been paying down your debt, and which now can be put to other uses.

Building the emergency fund to, say, three months' expenses is a really liberating place to be. Now you know that if you lose your job, you have a buffer to tide you over while you look for work. Or you know that if the boiler blows up and needs replacing, the money is there to pay for it.

I don't think there is a correct amount of money to have in an emergency fund; it depends on your circumstances and your feeling of security. I have one client who keeps £250,000 in her current account. This makes absolutely no financial sense as that money is earning nothing. But it provides peace of mind for my very nervous client. She's quite elderly and knows that a quarter of a million quid is probably more than she'll need for the rest of her life, which means she can afford to invest the rest of her estate for her children and grandchildren.

Find a level of security blanket that works for you. Whether it's £1,000, £5,000 or £20,000 will be a function of your feelings about risk, your job security, and your level of earnings and outgoings.

Build this emergency fund as quickly as you can by redirecting your debt snowball money once the debt has gone. You should keep this money accessible so that you can shift it into your current account at a moment's notice. An easy-access Cash ISA is a good bet, though that can be in just one person's name only, or you could opt for an online instant access account. Remember the point here is not to invest this money to earn a lot of interest; it's there for emergencies only.

Once you are debt-free, and have a comfortable buffer behind you, you are truly the master of your own financial destiny. Maybe for the first time, you're beholden to no one. You may still have a mortgage, but that's OK – that's a good debt.

Before we go any further, I need to go into a bit more detail about the principle that underpins the practice of spending less than you earn – *paying yourself first*.

Chapter 4
Pay Yourself First

THERE'S A PASSAGE IN THE *Bible* where Jesus says "Where your treasure is, there will your heart be also." In other words, whatever is most important to you, that's where you should prioritise your resources.

You should be your number one priority. I know that you have other things which are important to you, but your own financial peace and security ought to at the very top of that list.

The American humourist Will Rogers is quoted as saying, "Too many people spend money they haven't earned to buy things they don't want to impress people they don't like." I would add to this and say that we often buy stuff we don't need to make us feel better, even though that kind of retail therapy is very short-lived.

So often we relegate our financial future way down the list of priorities when it comes to planning our spending. Instead we take on debt, live for today and buy daft things. That makes no sense. If we truly are our own number one priority, we should be making sure that our needs are put before anything else. In other words, we should pay ourselves first.

That means we should be prioritising the improvement of our own financial situation above all else. It means deciding to eat in rather than out, if that means an extra £20 being paid off our debt. Paying off debt means that we'll soon be finished making other people rich, and have more of our money each month to save for our own future.

What does all this mean in practice? *Let's find out.*

Everything you need to KNOW

1. Paying yourself first means improving your own financial situation

When we are paying off debt, including interest, we are making other people richer, instead of ourselves. Every penny which is working for them is not working for us, and that's no good.

However, debt must be repaid, and that's why I still include paying down debt as paying yourself first. Even though technically it is paying someone else, it is improving your own financial situation.

Once the debt is cleared and the money is all yours to save and invest, that's even better. Now it's all in your hands, working for your future success.

When establishing your budget as detailed in Chapter 2, you should prioritise debt repayment and then saving above all else. Paying yourself first once again follows that principle of placing the big rocks in the jar first; everything else comes afterwards.

2. Saving what's left never works

As mentioned in Chapter 1, your saving cannot rely on money *left at the end of the month*, as the immutable laws of expenditure will mean there is no money left. Things will happen that will require you to spend money you weren't planning to, and those skinny lattes will add up. Before you know it, payday is three days away and you're running low on funds again.

Using your budget to pay yourself first is therefore a statement of intent. By identifying the money you will use to save or pay down debt before all other bills, you are declaring that you are the most important line on your budget, and that you will put yourself first above all else. It's being intentional in pursuing an independent financial future.

3. Your savings rate is a good measure of financial success

Your savings rate is a way of defining how much of your income you are paying yourself first, either by reducing debt or by saving for the future. You will see it defined in lots of different ways, but I like to keep things simple.

Add up your total debt repayments (excluding your mortgage) or your savings payments, and divide the total into your take-home monthly income.

For example, if your net monthly income is £2,000 per month, and you are either saving or repaying non-mortgage debt with £300 per month, that's a savings rate of 15%.

Is there an optimum savings rate? I don't think so – each person is different, with different goals and timescales. The obvious answer is that your savings rate should be as high as possible, but life should be enjoyed in the present as well as the future, and so finding a balance is important.

One rule of thumb might be to aim for a savings rate of your age minus 15. If you're 25 years old, you might aim for a savings rate of 10%. Notice I say *aim for* – you mustn't beat yourself up if you're not up to this level right from the start.

Remember, a rule of thumb is just that, and not a hard and fast rule. Anything is better than nothing – a 3% savings rate is better than 0%. As long as you make it your goal to increase your savings rate over time, your future self will thank you for it.

4. Defining short-, medium- and long-term savings

Now is a good opportunity to nail down what I mean by short-term, medium-term and long-term savings.

I define short-term saving as putting aside money you will need in the next year. For example, each month Joanne and I put aside money for Christmas. That's the definition of short term, as I know the money will be spent within 12 months. Saving for next year's holiday would also fall into the short-term category.

Medium-term savings are defined as two to five years out. Saving for a new car in three years' time would count as medium-term savings, as would saving towards an eternity ring for the big anniversary the year after next.

Finally, long-term savings is when you're working towards things five years or more in the future. For many of us, saving for retirement is a long term process, as is saving to help our kids through university.

Everything you need to DO

1. Set all debt repayments and savings to be paid the day after payday

Paying yourself first means paying yourself straightaway after you have been paid from work. For experienced budgeters, it doesn't really matter when in the month you pay your bills, but if you're just getting started, there's a lot to be said for setting things up for an easy win.

The two-account system of budgeting I described in Chapter 2 helps with this as you will make sure you leave enough in the Bills Account to cover everything.

For example, if you're paid on the 20th of each month, set your savings and debt payments to go out on the 21st or 22nd, to give chance for money to clear and weekends and bank holidays to get out of the way.

If you're paid on the last working day of the month, set your payments to go out on the first working day of the following month.

You may not be able to choose the date your debt repayments are made, but it is worth a try. Call or email your credit card or loan companies to see if they are flexible with this.

2. Make the most of any pay rises

When you get extra money from working, in the form of a promotion, pay rise or bonus, make sure the first thing you do is pay yourself first. This means taking a portion of that extra money and adding it to your savings.

This might require you to change standing order or direct debit amounts to increase them slightly. Remember that if you are currently saving 5% of your income, and you get a pay rise, your savings rate as a percentage of your income will be lower unless you also increase the savings amount you make.

Make a point of reassessing your savings and debt repayment strategy every time your income rises. Make it a part of your next monthly budget session after you have received the pay rise.

You may even be able to automate this process to some extent. Some pension and investment plans allow you to automatically increase your contributions each year. Call your providers to find out. It takes some of the decision-making away from you and this can sometimes be a good thing.

3. Harness the power of small increments

Small, incremental increases in your savings will make a significant difference over time. Here's an example.

Let's say you can save £100 per month, or £1200 per year, and you invest in such a way that your money grows by 5% per year, every year.

If you never increase the amount you save, over 25 years you will have invested £30,000 in total, and this will have grown to a value of £60,136.

Now let's say you increase your savings rate by £10 per month each year. So in year two, you will be saving £110 per month; in year three you will be saving £120 per month and so on. In this case, after 25 years you will have saved a total of £66,000 and this will have turned into £117,408.

Do you think that over that period of time you would notice an extra £10 per month each year? Definitely not. And yet what a difference it makes to the outcome! Let's take it a step further.

Now, rather than increase by £10 per month each year, you organise things so that each year you save 10% more than you did in the previous year.

This exponential increase in your savings rate will mean that over 25 years you will have saved £118,016, and this will have turned into £187,698.

4. Try the 13x multiplier

Back in the late 1990s when I worked for the Co-op Insurance Society, I got paid every four weeks, for some long-forgotten historical reasons. That meant I got paid 13 times each year.

Of course, all my monthly bills were still calendar-monthly, paid 12 times per year, so in effect, I got an extra payday each year – result! If only I'd had the presence of mind in my early 20s to put that money to good use.

What if I had paid my mortgage payment 13 times each year instead of 12? What difference would that have made?

Most of us are not in the position to be able to pay our mortgage twice in one month, but you may still be able to enjoy the benefit of making the equivalent of an extra mortgage payment each year. You can create a similar effect by dividing your monthly payment by 12, and then adding that amount to each of your monthly payments.

For example, if you have a £150,000 repayment mortgage, payable over 25 years with an interest rate of 3%, your monthly payment will be £711 per month. If we divide that £711 by 12, we get £59.25, so let's round that up to £60.

If you increase your normal monthly mortgage payment by that £60 you get a new monthly payment of £771. If you pay at this rate over 25 years, you will pay your mortgage off two years and nine months early, saving £7,690 in interest in the process.

It's a cool way of overpaying your mortgage each month in a way which you may not really notice the extra money going out. Of course, you can apply this to any debt repayment, not just to your mortgage.

Overpaying long-term debt can make huge difference over time. To see how much you can save on your mortgage by overpaying even small amounts, there's a fantastic mortgage overpayment calculator over at Money Saving Expert.[5]

---

[5] Find it at www.moneysavingexpert.com/mortgages/mortgage-over-payment-calculator.

Chapter 5
Dealing with Setbacks and Challenges

I HAVE A WEIRD THING THAT I do whenever I'm having any work done at the dentist. I always ask Craig, my softly-spoken Scottish dentist, to talk me through what they are going to do before they start and again as he begins each step of the process.

Why do I do this? It's so I can be prepared for what's coming. I like to know which parts of the procedure might hurt and which parts I can relax through. If I'm prepared beforehand, I can deal with what's coming.

The way I have laid out the practice of spending less than you earn, it sounds simple enough, right? And it *is* simple, but that doesn't make it easy.

Life has a way of making things harder for you than you want them to be. How you react to these challenges will define your success or otherwise.

What will you do? Will you fold at the first sign of any difficulty, when the first unexpected bill strikes? Or will you take a deep breath, pull out your budget and find a way to proceed? As with anything in life, being prepared is half the battle.

In this chapter you'll learn why bad things happen and how to deal with them.

Everything you need to KNOW

1. Shit happens

That's life. You might as well prepare for it now. Bad stuff is going to come your way to a greater or lesser extent.

If you know that, you can deal with it when it comes. OK? Good. Moving on…

2. Understand that we all have triggers

Regular listeners to my podcast know that I have, for all of my adult life, struggled with my weight. Of course, it isn't really my weight I battle against, it's my propensity to eat too much rubbish and exercise too little – I struggle with **myself**.

Notice how easy it is to offload the blame for something away from ourselves onto something or someone else. "It isn't me, it's my genes," or "My parents never taught be about money," and so on.

If you are reading this book because up to now you haven't been very good at managing your money, it is important to take a good hard look at why this has been the case.

Try taking a look at the last few items you bought that aren't groceries. Did you buy a gadget that you've never used or clothes you've never worn? Why do you think that was the case? What triggered you to make those purchases?

This might take a while, but it is worth being (that word again) very intentional when shopping. Do you buy more stuff when you're feeling tired or depressed? Is retail therapy an issue for you?

Once you have identified the triggers which lead to bad spending decisions, you can take steps to avoid those triggers where possible – more on that in a minute.

3. Budgeting difficulties come in different shapes and sizes

Remember back in Chapter 3 when we set up an emergency fund? Most of the things you have to deal with will not be so big as to derail you completely. For the most part, we're not talking about you being unable to work for two years because of a cancer diagnosis, or your partner dying early. That's what Section 2 is all about – protecting against *disaster*.

Most of us never have to deal with disaster, I'm pleased to say. For most people, the worst we have to deal with is an unexpected tax bill, or having to change all four tyres *and* the brake pads of the car, when we were expecting a routine service.

These are the kinds of things that your emergency fund is designed to shelter you against. In the past, they might have meant you getting further into debt, but with your emergency fund behind you, they can now be covered with ease.

Let's not panic about the really big stuff and try to get things in perspective, while all the time putting measures in place to protect ourselves.

Everything you need to DO

1. Don't panic!

Did anyone else hear Corporal Jones from *Dad's Army* when they read that?

When unexpected events happen, you need to keep your head. Getting into a flap and running around wondering what to do next won't help you at all.

It's never good to make hasty decisions in the heat of the moment. Very few events will require a decision from you in the space of a few minutes. At worst you'll have a few hours to get your head together, and more likely you'll have the time to think through your response carefully, sleeping on it before taking action.

Decide that you're going to take that time and use it wisely. Think through the implications of what has happened.

An unexpected bill has come in and it needs to be paid. Can you pay it out of this month's budget, or will you need to dip into your emergency fund? If you have more than one savings pot, which is the best place to take the money from? If you think you can pay the bill from income, what needs to be changed in your budget to make room for the unexpected item? Do you need to call your friends and cancel dinner this weekend to free up the money?

Breathe, stay calm, and execute. You've got this.

2. Take a long-term perspective

While the unexpected event can seem like a big deal in the moment, in the context of your long-term financial plan, it's just a blip on a very long timeline.

Now might be a good time to revisit your long-term goals and values that we talked about in the Money Mindset section. These are the reasons you want to get in financial shape and the things you want to achieve as a result of taking control over your money.

Pull out the notebook where you have your goals written down and take five minutes to go over them and get excited about them again. This will help you avoid getting into a slump when the road is rocky. Instead, it'll help you refocus and put your best foot forward.

3. Avoid your trigger situations

This won't always be easy, but once you have identified the trigger situations which lead to bad financial decisions, you can choose to avoid those situations where possible.

If you tend to buy stuff you don't need from Amazon at 11pm after two glasses of wine, consider turning off your laptop at 9pm and reading a book instead.

If you always go shopping the weekend after payday and find yourself spending too much, decide to go shopping in the last week of the month instead, and stick a note on your debit card with the clothing budget figure on it.

Do whatever it takes to break habits and activities which are unhelpful. Your future self will thank you for it.

4. Learn from your mistakes

Don't expect perfection from day one. Old habits die hard, and you're very likely to make some mistakes. When you do, don't beat yourself up endlessly. Instead, analyse the reasons for what happened, and try to learn from those reasons, so that you can avoid the situation next time.

Financial success is such a long-term game, it's way too much to expect that you should be 100% focused, 100% of the time. You're not a machine, you're a human, and as such you can expect to blow it from time to time.

That's OK, as long as you engage your superior human brain to learn from the mistakes in order to improve as you go along.

5. Pay back your emergency fund

If you have dipped into your emergency fund you need to top it back up using the same budgeting skills you used to build it up in the first place.

Treat the money you took out of your emergency fund as a loan to yourself. You could even pay yourself some interest on the money, or set a timescale for the fund to be topped back up.

You may need to pull back on your other savings for a couple of months or so, but the peace of mind of having the emergency fund full again will be worth it. And you can always pick up your regular savings where you left off.

We've covered some excellent ground in this section and there's lots more to come. By now you should have the following things sorted out:

⇨ Two bank accounts set up.

⇨ A solid monthly budget, looking ahead not backwards, which you have built and are sticking to.

⇨ An emergency fund in place or in the process of being built.

⇨ A clear plan for paying down your debt.

Spending less than you earn really is the core skill for financial success. Your ability to make good decisions about £10 or £100 here and there will serve you very well when, in the future, you have to make decisions over thousands, or even hundreds of thousands, of pounds.

If you can break free of debt by following the two account system, the budget planner, and rolling the debt snowball, and if you can keep on applying those principles by paying yourself first and increasing your savings rate over time, financial success is guaranteed.

But even if you do everything right, sometimes life throws you a **serious** curveball, with the potential to undo all your hard work.

Let's look at how you prevent that from throwing you off course and disrupting all your hard work in Step Two – Protect Against Disaster.

Step 2

Protect Against Disaster

THE SECOND OF THE THREE steps to financial success is all about protecting your financial future against disaster. We are talking about events which are truly shattering, such as dying early, suffering a life-changing illness, or being unable to work for a long period of time.

Each of these events has serious financial implications for you and your family, and your goals for your future may have to change as a result.

But it is possible to put in place some protection against the worst effects of these events. No amount of insurance will guarantee that you or your loved ones won't be diagnosed with cancer, but the **financial** effects of the worst-case scenario can be minimised with some thought and action up front.

The series of chapters in Step Two are designed to help you understand the key risks that you face, and the financial impact of those risks actually happening.

Then I will introduce you to the main kinds of insurance designed to help mitigate the impact of those risks, and help you work out how much cover you need for your specific circumstances.

Finally, we'll talk about the best way to make sure that your wishes are still carried out, even if you're no longer able to make financial decisions for yourself.

I know what you're thinking; this doesn't sound like the most uplifting of subjects. That's true, but part of taking control of our finances is facing up to potentially terrible things like an early death or serious diagnosis, and making sure that you have thought ahead and planned for these eventualities.

Please don't be tempted to skip this section. Maybe you never thought about this stuff before – that's often the case, particularly for younger people. But this is one of my three steps to financial success, not just a sidebar. It is just as important as the other two. Any financial plan which is missing this step is like a stool with only two legs – it just won't hold up under pressure.

Brace yourself, and let's get going.

Chapter 6
Lay a Solid Foundation

THERE'S A STORY IN THE *Bible* about two men who built houses for themselves. One man built his house on a foundation of solid rock:

> "The rain came down, the streams rose, and the winds blew and beat against that house; yet it did not fall, because it had its foundation on the rock."[6]

The other guy built his house on sand and let's just say that when the storm came, things didn't end well.

It's the same with our financial plans. We can have lofty goals and come up with a plan to attain them over time, but if disaster strikes and our foundations are made of sand, our whole financial lives can be ruined. To avoid this we need to lay a solid foundation of insurance.

The biggest problem with insurance is that it feels like money for nothing. If you never claim on an insurance policy, then you usually get nothing back. It feels like your money has just disappeared.

But I can tell you countless stories of people who have had insurance and resented paying it, right until they needed to claim. Like the chap

---

6   Matthew 7:25, New International Version of the *Bible*.

who sat in my office and said that he wanted to cancel his critical illness policy (I explain more about those very soon). In fact, several times over the years he thought about cancelling and I always managed to talk him out of it.

A little over a year ago, he was diagnosed with cancer and, thanks to the insurance policy, was able to pay off his mortgage and take as much time as he needed to get well, without having to worry about paying the bills.

Everything you need to KNOW

1. How insurance works

Insurance works on a few basic principles.

One is that **the premiums (payments) of the many pay for the claims of the few**. For all the millions of people that pay for car insurance each year, only a small proportion of those will make a claim. That keeps everyone's premiums manageable and is the reason why when the insurers get more claims in one year, premiums tend to rise the following year.

Second, insurance is always agreed between the insurer and the customer on a principle of **utmost good faith**. This old-fashioned sounding phrase means that when you apply for insurance of any kind, the insurer assumes you're telling the truth, and you have to declare that you're doing so. If it turns out that you have lied on the application form, your insurance may end up being void.

For their part, the insurer has to provide you with everything you need to know to make an informed decision about whether the insurance is right for you. That goes for middle-men too, such as financial advisers or insurance brokers.

Finally, there needs to be something called **insurable interest**. This means that the person taking out the insurance must stand to lose out if the insured event happens. I can't take out life insurance on, say, Lewis Hamilton the Formula One racing driver, because I don't stand to be any worse off if he dies. But I can take out insurance on the lives of my business partners, or my wife, because I will be affected financially if they die.

This extends to the fact that you can't take out insurance on a child's life.

2. Assurance vs Insurance

When I went to financial adviser school,[7] they taught me that you took out **assurance** for something which can't be replaced, like a life, and **insurance** for things that can be replaced, like a car or house.

These days, the word assurance tends to be used more by professionals and sounds old-fashioned to me. I'm trying to get into the habit of using the word insurance for everything.

3. The three major risks

When it comes to impacting your financial future, there are three major risks that you can insure against:

1. Early death

2. Diagnosis and survival of a critical illness like cancer or a heart attack

3. Inability to work due to accident or illness

In the next three chapters we'll get into more detail about each of these events and the insurance you can take out to protect against them. But you may have spotted a glaring omission from this list. What about losing your job by being made redundant – surely that will have an impact on your financial future?

Indeed it will, but unemployment insurance is notoriously expensive and difficult to claim upon. For this reason, I haven't recommended it

---

[7]   There isn't really such a place; I learnt on the job.

to clients for nearly 20 years. It's far better to prepare for this particular eventuality by ensuring you have an adequate emergency fund in place, and good budget controls too. Of course, by the time you've read this far, that's second nature to you, right?

Everything you need to DO

1. Establish the financial impact of a loss

Before we get into the detail of the three major types of insurance you should consider, it helps to try to quantify the financial impact of these three major events.

When you think about it, each of them represents the loss of the person's biggest financial asset – their income. Take someone who aged 22 starts their career earning £20,000 per year. Let's say they never get a promotion or pay rise, just a 3% increase each year to keep pace with inflation. Over a 43-year career to age 65, they will have earned a total of just over £1.7 million.

Now let's say that every five years this person gets a promotion and a 10% pay rise, as well as the 3% increment. In this case, they will earn just over £2.7million over their 43 years of working life.

Most of us will never own a house or anything else valued at these amounts. Therefore, our ability to earn an income is indeed our most valuable asset, and it can be severely impacted by early death, serious illness or incapacity.

I know this doesn't sound like fun, but you should spend some time to establish the impact of these events.

Debt

Firstly, what would happen to any debt that you have? If you are single and you die, you'll no longer be around to care, but that doesn't mean the debt is wiped off. No, your estate will have to pay it and if you don't have enough money or assets to cover the debt, your creditors may look to the beneficiaries of your estate, usually your family members, to make up the difference.

In a couple, would the survivor be able to keep paying the debt if their partner were to die? If the survivor is the major breadwinner, then maybe they would. But if the wife is earning £100,000 per year and the husband is earning £30,000 per year, and between them they have a mortgage of £300,000, if the wife dies, the husband is going to struggle.

Conventional wisdom says that ideally any major debts such as a mortgage should be paid off in the event of the death of the borrower – life insurance can be used to achieve this. Critical illness insurance can also be used to pay off the debt if one of the borrowers is diagnosed with one of the listed illnesses, more of which in Chapter 8.

Regular outgoings

It makes sense to make some provision to pay off major debt if one of the events happens, but most bills would continue. All the costs of owning or renting a property would continue, as would extra costs if you have kids, and the obvious things like food for the family, etc. None of these costs disappear if you can't work.

A good exercise is to look at your total outgoings and work out what your essential outgoings are. These are things that you simply must pay in order to survive and would include your mortgage or rent and all the other bills associated with running a household, plus food of course.

It would not include eating out, entertainment, club memberships or your Sky TV subscription. You might joke to your friends that you couldn't do without Sky Sports, but if you really had to, of course you could.

When you have stripped everything unnecessary out of your budget, ask yourself: would you be able to sustain this standard of living on one salary, if you're in a couple? Or if you're single and were not able to work, how long could you live like this based on the savings you have put aside?

For many of us this will be a sobering exercise and will highlight just how exposed we are if we lose our income.

We'll look at how to insure against the three major events in the next three chapters. After that we'll learn how to put together a cohesive protection programme so you can rest easy, reassured that if the very worst happens, your financial life should be able to stay broadly on track.

Chapter 7
Life Insurance

PREMATURE DEATH IS THE MOST traumatic and final of our three insurable events. That's why so many people never consider the impact of their own death. After all, it doesn't make for a pleasant evening's activity: "I know what we can do this evening darling – let's crack open a bottle of Merlot and talk about the financial impact of one of us dying!"

None of us likes to consider our own mortality, but if we're dead, we won't be around to worry about things anymore. It is the impact on those left behind that should be the focus of our attention.

We should look to minimise their financial worries at a time which is already going to be incredibly traumatic. After all, can you imagine your partner or your parents having to deal with bailiffs or debt collectors while grieving for you? Fortunately, it is easy to make sure this doesn't happen.

Everything you need to KNOW

1. Terminology

We need to define some terms at the outset here, because as you set up different kinds of insurance, you're going to read and hear these terms and you need to understand them.

⇨ **Life insured** – the person on whose life the insurance is taken out. If this person dies, the insurance pays out.

⇨ **Sum insured** – the amount that will be paid out if the life insured dies. (By the way, you may also see the slightly different terms **life assured** and **sum assured** – they mean the same thing.)

⇨ **Premium** – the monthly or annual cost of the insurance policy.

⇨ **Term** – the length of time the policy lasts.

⇨ **Life of another** – a policy can be owned by the person who is the life insured, called an own-life policy, or by someone else, as long as insurable interest exists between the two parties. The most common example of this in practice is where one partner owns an insurance policy on the life of the other.

2. Types of life insurance

Life insurance can be broadly divided into two main types, each of which has a few sub-types. Stay with me – this is important.

Term insurance

Term insurance, as the name suggests, insures the life for a fixed term. Most insurance is term insurance. Think of your car insurance – you renew it every year, so each policy has a term of one year.

With life insurance, the policy will pay out the sum insured if the life insured dies within the term. If they survive the whole term of the policy, then die the day after, nothing will be paid out. That might sound harsh, but again, consider your car insurance. If you don't have an accident during the year, the policy pays out nothing.

Because the sum insured will only pay out during a fixed term, this makes it easier for the insurance companies to work out the chance of them having to pay out on the policy. The insurers have tables showing how likely an average 40-year-old man is to die before he reaches age 60. From this information, they can work out the cost of providing life insurance on that basis.

Only a few 40-year-old men will die before they are 60, but a far greater number will die before they reach age 80. Therefore, a 20-year life term life insurance policy will be much cheaper than a 40-year policy, as it is less likely to pay out.

Needless to say, the life insurance companies are in it to make a profit, and that's a good thing, because if they go bust, all our policies would be worthless!

Types of term insurance

There are three main types of term life insurance that you need to be aware of:

1. **Level term** – the sum insured stays level throughout the term. If you die on day one of the policy or on the very last day, the payout will be the same.

2. **Decreasing term** – the sum insured decreases throughout the term. This kind of policy is often used to protect a repayment mortgage, where the amount of debt outstanding reduces over the life of the mortgage.

3. **Family income benefit (FIB)** – a kind of decreasing term insurance, an FIB policy pays out a regular income, rather than a lump sum. Sometimes it can be unhelpful to drop a large amount of money on a surviving partner, when perhaps a regular annual amount might be more manageable.

Each of these serves a purpose and is better suited to different situations and people.

Whole of life insurance

The main alternative to term insurance is whole of life insurance. Again, these kinds of policies have been intelligently named, as in this case the policy lasts for the whole of the life insured's life, no matter how long.

Think back to our earlier discussion about the premiums being set by the life insurance companies based on the likelihood of the life insured dying. Given that everyone dies eventually, wouldn't this make whole of life insurance very expensive?

Yes, it does, but there are more factors involved than just the 100% likelihood of death. Firstly, not everyone keeps a policy for its full duration. Financial hardship might make some people cancel their policies, for example.

Also, there are different ways of arranging whole of life insurance which also affect the premium level.

Guaranteed cover or not?

The simplest kind of whole of life cover works similarly to a level term insurance, but has no end date. The premium stays the same, the sum insured stays the same and everything is very simple and straightforward.

But the premiums for this kind of insurance are relatively high and beyond the reach of many people. Necessity is always the mother of invention and so the life insurance companies looked for ways to reduce the premiums, making whole of life cover more accessible for more people.

One way they did this was to introduce an element of investment. Part of each premium is used to pay for the insurance and another part is invested by the life insurance company. The thinking here is that the growth in the invested part will help subsidise the cost of the life cover part. The life company also makes a fee on the investment part which further allows them to reduce the premium.

In addition to the introduction of investment-backed insurance, the life insurance companies offered a low starting rate of premium which would be reviewed every ten years or sometimes more often. At review, the life insurance company would consider all factors such as claims history, changes to the death rate and investment returns in order to determine whether the premiums should rise.

I have seen instances where premiums have quadrupled at review, making a previously affordable policy completely prohibitive. My issue with reviewable insurance is that it is very hard for a layperson to understand what the criteria for review are, and in any case, they couldn't hope to influence the process. They are completely at the mercy of the insurance company, which is never a good place to be.

For this reason, I urge you to avoid whole of life cover which involves any element of investment or review. Instead, stick to the (admittedly more expensive) guaranteed kind. At least you know where you are, and over time, the premiums become less expensive thanks to inflation.

3. Underwriting

This term came from the original insurance policies where the people offering the insurance would literally write their names under the terms of the policy. These days it means the process of assessing your suitability for the policy, from the insurance company's point of view.

When you complete an application for a life insurance policy, you are asking the insurance company to consider insuring you. They will assess the details you have put on the form to determine the terms they are prepared to offer you.

Sometimes they will ask you for more information and may write to your doctor or even ask you to go for a medical. This whole process is called underwriting and ends up with one of three outcomes:

I. **Acceptance at ordinary rates** – each life insurance company publishes the standard terms they will offer to a healthy person of your age and sex. If everything on your application stacks up, you will be offered these published rates.

2. **Acceptance at higher rates or with exclusions** – sometimes the life insurance company will decide that the risk to them is higher than normal and offer you the insurance but at a higher premium. Or sometimes they will keep the premium the same but exclude death for a specific reason. For example, maybe you have experienced depression in the past. The insurer may offer you ordinary rates but will not pay out if you take your own life.

3. **Decline** – the life insurance company declines to insure you. The most common reason for this outcome is if you have had serious medical issues in the past and survived. Your risk of dying is therefore much higher than someone who has not suffered those issues, and the insurer may take the view that the risk is too high for them to consider.

Everything you need to DO

1. Establish the right kind of cover for your needs

Now that you know how the different kinds of insurance work, you can decide which kind of policy might suit your situation best.

If you have a significant debt like a repayment mortgage, a decreasing term policy would work best. The sum insured reduces over the term, but so does the outstanding balance of the mortgage. Make sure your policy matches the **term** of the mortgage and also that the **rate of reduction** in the sum insured matches the rate of mortgage repayment.

Once your major debt is covered, decide what protection you might need for those left behind. If you're single, the answer might be zero. If you're in a couple or have a family, then you should definitely make some provision for them if you die. Decide whether that should be in the form of a lump sum from a level term policy, or a regular annual payment from a family income benefit policy.

2. Determine how much cover you need

Work out how much would be a good amount to insure. That can be tricky to pin down, but will often come down to a compromise between a high level of cover and affordable monthly premiums. I might want to provide £2 million of insurance for my wife, but if it costs me £500 per month, I'll need to set my sights somewhat lower.

If I were to die, then for my wife and kids, life goes on. Joanne might meet someone else, or she might return to work full-time and earn enough to support the family by herself. The right amount of life cover will probably focus on easing the financial difficulty in the immediate aftermath of your death, rather than making sure your partner and kids are financially comfortable forever. Chances are the latter won't be affordable for you anyway.

You should consider the term here too. For example, I have some life insurance which will run out when my youngest daughter reaches age 25; the thinking is that both kids should be independent by then and so my death will have less of an impact on the family. Joanne won't have the tie of the kids after that point and so can support herself far more easily.

Make sure you take into account any life insurance benefits payable to you from your employer. Some companies have very generous **death-in-service** schemes, which are life insurance policies themselves. Usually the sum insured is expressed as a multiple of your earnings and you'll probably get something once a year from the HR department letting you know what the amount of cover is.

You could consider this to be extra to the life cover you take out yourself. Remember, if you move jobs, your future employer may not offer such a benefit, or they could offer more cover. As you're not in control of this, be careful not to rely completely on death-in-service cover.

As you can see, there's no right answer here; there is no optimum amount of life insurance you should take out. Instead, try to find a balance that works for you. Having said that, here are some guidelines:

1. **Single person** – take out term life cover to make sure your major debts are paid off. Or take out an amount of cover so your estate can keep up the repayments on that debt until, for example, your house can be sold to clear the debt. You probably don't need much more than this unless you have kids – see below.

2. **In a couple** – cover the major debts and provide an extra sum or income benefit to cushion the blow of your death. Take your individual situation into account. If the survivor is likely to struggle financially due to low earnings power, for example, then provide more cover than if they are likely to be able to support themselves comfortably.

3. **With kids** – make extra provision to compensate the children for the loss of your financial input over their childhood. You might want to provide a sum to help them through university, or onto the housing ladder, or even just to buy their first car.

Again, compromise is likely to be the order of the day here. Start with what you would want to provide and get some quotes from a financial adviser or a comparison site to see if they are affordable. If not, decide how you will compromise until you come up with a total cost which works for you.

There is more on this in Chapter 10, where I show you how to put together a programme of insurance for you and your family.

Chapter 8
Critical Illness Insurance

IF YOU DIE EARLY, IT is those left behind that have to pick up the pieces of their lives and finances in your absence. But if you are diagnosed with a critical illness, you're very much still in the picture, and have to experience the financial implications yourself.

It may also be the case that your diagnosis means that your life will change in other ways, such as having to adapt your home for mobility reasons, or having to attend dialysis four times a week. If that were that case, can you imagine your financial situation remaining the same as it is now?

Rather, your earnings power is likely to be seriously impacted, and remember, your mortgage and other commitments still have to be paid.

These days, thanks to advances in medical treatment and care, you are more likely to survive many of the so-called critical illnesses, and therefore insurance to cover them is an important part of any comprehensive financial plan.

Everything you need to KNOW

1. What is a critical illness?

Critical illness insurance used to be called *dread disease* cover back in the day, but the name has been changed because it now covers much more than a few serious diseases.

At its most basic, critical illness cover pays out a lump sum on the diagnosis of cancer, heart attack or stroke. Of course, there are many different types of cancer and severities of stroke, so we need to dig a little deeper.

The Association of British Insurers has a core list of conditions, as follows:

⇨ Cancer

⇨ Coronary artery bypass surgery

⇨ Heart attack

⇨ Kidney failure

⇨ Major organ transplant

⇨ Multiple sclerosis

⇨ Stroke

These are the conditions that are statistically most likely to happen and as such you can expect to find them on every critical illness policy.

In addition, there is a list of additional conditions which may be covered:

⇨ Aorta graft surgery

⇨ Benign brain tumour

⇨ Blindness

⇨ Coma

⇨ Deafness

⇨ Heart valve replacement or repair

⇨ Loss of limbs

⇨ Loss of speech

⇨ Motor neurone disease

⇨ Paralysis/paraplegia

⇨ Parkinson's disease

⇨ Terminal illness

⇨ Third degree burns

If you are diagnosed with one of these conditions, according to the specific definitions in your policy, the sum insured will be paid out.

Usually part of the policy wording is that you have to **survive** for a defined period from diagnosis, usually 14 days. That might sound like no big deal, but it means that if, say, you were involved in a car accident and lost both your legs, and then died a week later from a complication, the policy may not pay out.

Finally, critical illness insurance is usually written on a term basis, meaning that if you are not diagnosed with one of the conditions within the term, you'll get nothing back from the policy.

2. Critical illness and life insurance often go together

Critical illness cover can be obtained as a stand-alone policy, but far more often it is tacked on to a life insurance policy in one of two ways.

Firstly, **accelerated** cover means that if the critical illness element of a policy pays out, then the policy has done its job and will finish at that point. If you never make a claim on the critical illness part of the policy, then the life cover element will pay out if you die. It's an either/ or situation – the sum insured will be paid on one or the other event, but not both.

The alternative is **additional** cover, where the critical illness cover is paid out as well as the life cover – they are separate events covered by one policy.

There's an added twist to this distinction. If you make a claim under the critical illness part of an accelerated cover policy, it is sometimes possible to **buy back** the life cover element of the policy without any further medical underwriting. This essentially turns an accelerated policy into an additional cover policy. If this is something that is likely to be important to you, I would opt for an additional policy from the outset, budget permitting.

Everything you need to DO

1. Establish whether critical illness insurance is a priority

While the optimum solution is to take out insurance for all three of the events – early death, critical illness, inability to work – in reality your budget might not permit that. If so, then you're going to need to prioritise.

Read the next chapter first, where I talk about income protection insurance, and decide for your situation which of the two types of policy might be the bigger priority.

2. Decide what level of cover you might need

Once again, this is likely to require some compromise, but always start high and work back from there.

The ideal would be that any major debts such as a mortgage would be paid off in full in the event of a critical illness diagnosis.

One compromise that I often recommend to my clients if full cover is too expensive, is to take out insurance to cover, say, three to five years of mortgage payments. This would give you a buffer period and a chance to recover from the illness. This solution will also be much cheaper.

Again, try and match the term of the policy to the debt it is intended to cover.

3. Drill down into the definitions

Make sure you truly understand the fine print of any policy before you take it out. It won't be a stimulating hour for you, but it is time well spent.

I can recall at least two occasions in my career where I have helped people claim on a policy they had, but didn't fully understand. They paid the premiums every month without thinking about it, but didn't know what they had. On another occasion, the time for making a claim had lapsed and so the policyholder missed their opportunity to claim – a disaster.

But that's not going to be you, because you're being intentional about all aspects of your money from now on.

And really, that's it. You can ask a financial adviser to help you take out critical illness cover, or you can use one of the many comparison websites such as CompareTheMarket.com or MoneySupermarket.com, just as you would when insuring your house or car. A good halfway house between these two routes is LifeSearch.co.uk, which offers specialist advice in this area.

Chapter 9
Income Protection Insurance

PERHAPS THE LEAST UNDERSTOOD, BUT potentially the most valuable kind of insurance, is income protection insurance.

This is another plan which used to suffer an image problem, like dread disease insurance. Income protection used to be called Permanent Health Insurance or PHI, which doesn't mean anything to ordinary people like you and me.

Income protection is designed to replace part of your income if you are unable to work through illness or injury. As with all insurance, though, it isn't quite as simple as that.

Everything you need to KNOW

1. Income Protection versus Accident, Sickness and Unemployment cover

Let me clear up one common point of confusion. Income protection cover is not designed to pay out if you lose your job due to being made redundant. It is only designed to pay out if you cannot work due to illness or injury.

The confusion arises because unemployment cover is sometimes called Accident, Sickness and Unemployment insurance (ASU). Hence it has an element of ill-health protection, but not in the same league as proper income protection cover.

As I mentioned earlier, ASU cover is expensive, very difficult to claim upon and only pays out for a short period of time, usually a year. Proper income protection may not include redundancy cover, but it will pay out until you return to work, however long that is, or until the end of the term.

I suggest you avoid Accident, Sickness and Unemployment insurance, and instead look for a decent income protection policy. You can protect yourself against redundancy by having a decent emergency fund in place.

2. Definitions of incapacity

Surely being unable to work is pretty straightforward? Either you can work or you can't, right?

Nope. Insurers use three main definitions of what it means to be incapable of working:

1. **Own occupation** – this means the policy will pay out if you are unable to do the job you were doing immediately before the claim.

2. **Any occupation** – here, the policy will pay out if you are unable to do your own job, or any other job to which you are suited by your qualifications or experience.

3. **Activities of daily living** – in this case, a policy would pay out if you are unable to complete two or three from a list of standard daily activities, such as feeding yourself, dressing, or going to the toilet unaided.

These three definitions of incapacity are in order of likelihood of pay out. You are far more likely to be unable to do your specific job, than you are of being so badly incapacitated that you can't feed yourself. That means that an own occupation definition is a better quality of policy and is therefore likely to be the most expensive.

As usual, each insurer may have slightly different wordings of these definitions. Again, it's on you to dig deep and find out if the policy you are considering will cover you to the extent that you want.

As you can imagine, certain occupations are riskier than others. I spend my working hours sitting at a desk, where the worst thing that is likely to happen is that I fall off my chair. A scaffolder, by contrast, works at heights and does a manual job, with a much greater chance of being injured.

Insurance companies group occupations into classes from low risk to high risk, and unsurprisingly offer cheaper premiums to those in lower-risk jobs.

3. Deferred periods and linked claims

When you make a claim on an income protection policy, a clock starts ticking, counting down the **deferred period**. If you are able to return to work before the deferred period ends, then the policy will not pay out, simple as that.

The longer the deferred period, the less likely you are to claim, and therefore the cheaper the policy will be. Deferred periods therefore serve two purposes. One is that you can design your policy around your sick benefits from work, or around your emergency fund – more of which shortly. Also, you can choose to opt for a longer deferred period to keep the cost of the policy within your budget.

What if you make a claim and the policy pays out, and then you return to work? An income protection policy will pay until you return to work, or until the end of the policy, whichever is sooner. When you take out a policy, you set the end date, which might coincide with your intended retirement age, your state pension age or the point at which you will have finished paying off your mortgage.

If the policy is paying out and then you recover and return to work, the policy will stop paying you when your salary recommences.

What if you then suffer a relapse of the same reason you were off sick the first time? Usually, this would be treated as a **linked claim** as long as it is within a certain period, say 12 months of the end of the first claim. In this case, the insurance company would waive the deferred period and the policy would begin paying out again immediately. If you are off work due to a different illness or injury, the deferred period would apply once again.

4. Cover limits and indexation

It isn't possible to cover 100% of your pre-illness earnings. Generally, the maximum cover is about 70% of your gross earnings from before you were unable to work.

But income protection benefits are tax free, so you would keep every penny of the claim income, as opposed to paying tax and national insurance on your earnings. In the end, your policy benefits wouldn't look too dissimilar from your pre-claim earnings.

You can set both the premiums and the benefits to rise with inflation. That way, you can take out a policy which is sufficient for your current needs and which should remain so, all other things being equal.

As ever, you should be intentional about keeping your insurance cover under review. If you receive a promotion, or your job changes, then you need to inform your insurance company and maintain the right level of cover.

5. What about the self-employed?

When you're working for someone else, it is fairly easy to define what it means to be off work, but when you're your own boss, the lines between home and work can be blurry. We are far more likely to drag ourselves to work because we're dependent on ourselves and no one else for our livelihood.

Sometimes the way self-employed people pay themselves is different to employees, too. If you own a limited company, it is often more tax-efficient to pay yourself a smaller salary and a larger dividend. But as the dividend is based on the profitability of the company, would you be able to take a dividend if you couldn't work?

Take me as an example. I own shares in and manage a firm of 16 people. I have three co-owners and 13 staff who could carry on the work pretty well if I was sick for an extended period of time. Therefore, my dividend income from the company is likely to continue – so would an income protection policy pay out?

Compare that with someone who is a one-person company, or a true self-employed person where if they don't work, zero money comes in the door. That's a much easier situation to define when that person goes off sick.

There's a rabbit hole of a discussion we could go down at this point, all about business owners and key-person protection, but that's really beyond the scope of this book. All I would suggest is that if you are in business for yourself, you should talk to a good accountant about the financial risks to the business and a financial adviser who is an expert in this field. Between those two professionals, they should set you in the right direction.

In the spirit of utmost good faith, it is important to be clear with the insurance company about how your income is made up, so that the cover can be tailored correctly.

Everything you need to DO

1. Establish how much cover you need

If you work for someone else, you need to be clear about **how long** they would pay you for if you were unable to work long-term. Is it one week, one month, six months, or longer? Public sector workers often get a better deal on sick benefits than private sector employees. Make sure you get this in writing – it'll be in your employment contract.

There may also be a limit on **how much** your employer will pay you. For example, it is common for long-term NHS employees to receive six months full pay and six months half pay if they are sick for an extended period.

Take existing sick benefits into account when working out your ideal level of income protection cover.

2. Establish the ideal deferred period

In the same way, you can plan your policy deferred period around your sick benefits from work and any emergency fund you may have put away. If you have erred on the high side for your emergency fund and have six months of expenses put away, then you can opt for a longer deferred period, knowing your own safety net will tide you over till the policy kicks in.

3. Take your essential and your desired expenses into account

Remember when you wrote down your minimum level of expenses you would have to pay out in order merely to survive? You can use that as a minimum benchmark for establishing income protection benefits, especially if budget constraints are a problem. You may not be able to afford the maximum cover available, but could settle for a more affordable lower amount.

Again, a financial adviser can help you to take out income protection insurance or you can search and apply through the many websites of the insurers that offer such services.

Chapter 10
Building a Protection Programme

NOW THAT YOU UNDERSTAND THE key risks that can derail your financial future, and the main insurance products you can use to mitigate the risks, how do you put it all together?

If money was no object, you would just take out loads of insurance cover for each of the three events and then move onto the next step. In practice though, you will have a limited budget and so you will need to compromise somehow.

In this chapter I help you do this by talking through how you can determine your priorities depending on your stage of life. Then we look at how to apply for insurance products and how to keep records of the insurance you have taken out.

Everything you need to KNOW

1. Decide your priorities

As I've mentioned several times, there is inevitably going to be some compromise involved in building a decent protection programme. Usually the compromise is between the ideal level of cover and the cost of providing it.

Deciding the order in which you address the three risks is largely down to your life-stage.

For example, if you are a single person with no financial dependents, you could argue that you have no need for life insurance. You may want to provide some money to your parents or other family members who may need to sort things out for you after you have gone. You may want to pay off your mortgage so your house can be left to your best mate. It's your call, but your need for life cover is lower than for someone with large debts and a family.

Here are my suggestions for the order of priority for different life stages.

Young (or old!), free and single

You should protect your income, first and foremost. Take out the maximum level of income protection insurance you can afford.

If you have a mortgage, try to cover it with a critical illness policy, or if that is prohibitive, arrange a policy with a sum insured of three to five years of mortgage payments, so you have a good buffer of cash behind you if you are diagnosed with something nasty. Consider doing this in conjunction with term life insurance as the extra cost will be minimal.

Double income, no kids yet (DINKYs)

Your first priority should be to soften the blow for the survivor if one of you were to die. The amount of cover could depend on the relative earnings of each partner. If one partner earns significantly more than the other, you might want to weight the sum insured accordingly.

At the very least, this should include paying off any large joint debts, such as a mortgage. Then provide an extra amount as a lump sum using term insurance or family income benefit to provide a financial cushion for the initial grieving period.

Then you should protect your incomes. If one partner earns significantly more than the other then their income should be protected first.

Finally, consider critical illness insurance for either the full amount of any joint debt, or a few years of payments as a compromise.

Young family

If you have kids, you should consider all the same things as the DINKYs above, but definitely add in some family income benefit with a term lasting at least until the kids reach age 18, and longer if you have designs on them going onto higher education.

You may also want to provide a small lump sum which can be theirs when they reach adulthood. To do this you will want to consider using a trust, of which more in the next chapter.

Empty nest

After the children have grown and left, your financial situation is likely to be better, and your debt is hopefully reducing. As a result, your need for insurance is probably reducing too.

Don't neglect income protection at this time. Usually at this point, you will be reaching your peak earnings years, and a long-term illness can completely muck up your plans for a comfortable retirement. Income protection will at least continue to provide you with a regular income stream until you would have retired.

At this point you could consider using life cover to redress any imbalance between your retirement provision. For example, if the female partner has gaps in her pension record due to a career break to raise children, you may want to consider this when choosing life insurance levels. A lump sum which could be invested to make up the difference would be helpful.

As you get older, all personal insurance gets more expensive, so now is a good opportunity to get things in order for the rest of your life, particularly if you are in good health.

2. Menu policies are a good idea

Look for so-called menu policies to make your life a little easier. These are one-stop-shop policies where you can arrange all three types of cover within one plan. This makes for one direct debit payment going out each month, making it easier to stay on top of your outgoings.

These plans often provide the opportunity to increase cover based on certain events like having more children or moving to a new house, without having to undergo medical underwriting again, which is a bonus.

The main benefit however is convenience.

3. Understand waiver of premium

Waiver of premium is an insurance for your insurance! It works like this: if you are unable to work due to accident or illness, usually for a period of six months or more, the premiums on your life insurance will stop until you return to work. They are paid for by the waiver of premium insurance.

As this insurance is based on your ability to do your job, you will find that some policies don't allow waiver to be added for some high-risk occupations.

As a rule, your default choice should be to add waiver of premium to any policy you take out. However, if you are self-employed with highly variable income, you may find it difficult to claim. If in doubt, talk to the insurance company you are dealing with, your broker or your financial adviser.

4. Understand policy ownership

If you are part of a couple, you also need to think about policy ownership. For most couples, a joint life insurance policy does the trick. It pays out on the first death, usually, and the proceeds pay out to the survivor. But if you have two single life policies, you can opt for a **life of another** basis. This simply means that I would own the policy on my wife's life, and she would own the one on my life.

What's the big deal here? If I own my own life insurance policy, then the proceeds of the policy would be paid out to my estate and would be distributed according to the terms of my will. As we'll learn in the next chapter, the process of gaining a grant of probate which allows the executors to distribute the estate can take a while. Most people take out life insurance to provide an immediate cushion of money for those left behind, and a nine-month wait for probate may not be good enough.

Opting for life of another policy ownership fixes this and provides for a quick pay out to the person who needs the money the most. More on this important subject in the next chapter.

Everything you need to DO

1. Get some quotes and apply

Once you have decided on an ideal amount and type of cover, you need to get some idea about what this will cost.

Most cost comparison websites will offer this service, but I suggest that you try a specialist insurance broker like LifeSearch.co.uk. Life insurance is one of the areas of personal finance where it is still legal for advisers and brokers to receive commissions from insurance companies, and in this case, I think that works well. It means that you can get advice which is free to you, as the adviser is remunerated by the commission. Of course, the commission is still paid indirectly by you, included in the premiums.

An alternative is to pay a fee to an adviser or broker, but make sure you're not doing both – so the adviser receives both a fee and a commission. If you are paying a fee, ask your adviser to rebate all commissions into the policy – it should bring the premiums down.

The adviser must show you why they are recommending a particular provider and policy. Obviously, it can't be because it's the plan that pays them the highest commission! They have to show that they have considered your needs and objectives, and why the recommended plan meets these.

You may prefer to fly solo and do all your own research and apply directly. Be aware that if you apply via a cost-comparison website, the site will be getting a commission for the sale.

For me, one of the key benefits in using a professional adviser here is that they will do all the applications and paperwork for you. I can tell you from long experience that filling in the application form for life insurance is a drag, but that's still the easy part! Once the forms have gone off, there can be lots of toing and froing between you, the insurer, and often your GP or medical assessment nurses. It's a hassle and having someone do that for you is money well spent.

2. Make a one-page record of what you have taken out

Most of us, when we have ticked off a big task like sorting out our insurance programme, tend to forget about it and move on to the next thing. But before you do that, I suggest you take stock and write a one-page summary of the insurance you have taken out.

The reason for this is simply that we soon forget what we took out and that's not a good way to be intentional about our finances. Your adviser, if you used one, will have provided a document with his or her proposed solutions, and may even have followed up after the event with a summary. But I have known it sometimes to take a few months to complete a round of underwriting, and people have short memories.

Take a sheet of paper and write on it "If I die, then…" and fill in the blank. It could read:

> "If I die, a lump sum of £250,000 will be paid out to Joanne from policy number ABC12345678 from XYZ Life Insurance Co."

or:

> "If I am unable to work due to accident or illness, I have an income protection policy with ABC Insurance Co, policy number XYZ87654321, which will pay me £2,000 per month, rising at the rate of inflation, after I have been off sick for 13 weeks."

Write a sentence for each plan that you take out, so that you or your loved ones know exactly what the deal is.

Then keep the policy documents you are given by the insurer with this piece of paper, so that everything is in one place. I suggest you take photocopies of all these documents and give them to someone you trust, the executor of your will perhaps, and ask them to keep them safe. Having a digital record stored in the cloud also makes sense.

3. Review your protection programme regularly

When you take out insurance cover, you do so based on your current debt, family situation, income levels, etc. All these will change over time and your insurance programme should change too.

I suggest that you get into the habit of sitting down once a year to assess your policies to ensure they remain fit for purpose. Take out the one-page summary you wrote and see if the programme still does the job for you. Now imagine if you had to sift through 40-odd pages of three different policy documents to do this and you'll thank me for making you draw up that one-pager!

If you think you could do with increasing or decreasing the cover, you should approach your insurer to see what terms they would offer and the process for securing them. Would they need further medical underwriting? What would the cost be? You can then compare these with the open market once again, or revisit your adviser.

If an event happens like a significant promotion, a change in relationship or a new baby, then that should be a trigger for a review.

It is important to be as intentional about your protection programme as it is about your budget and, as we'll see in Step Three, about your investments. Don't let your insurance policies languish in a filing drawer. Pull them out once a year to make sure they are still doing the job you need them to do.

Chapter 11
Wills, Trusts and Powers of Attorney

I**F WE WERE TO DIE** or become incapacitated in some way, we want to know that the process of sorting things out is as easy as possible for our loved ones. It isn't enough to provide financial support in the form of insurance – we also need to see to the practical arrangements as much as possible.

In doing so, you need to understand the processes of claiming on the various kinds of insurance, and also the legal framework for what happens when you die, or if you can't make your own decisions any more.

Remember that this book is not intended as an exhaustive guide, but merely to give you everything you need to know and everything you need to do to get yourself on a good footing. I suggest that when you have read this chapter and determined the steps you need to take, you should seek advice from a solicitor about how best to structure this aspect of your financial affairs.

Everything you need to KNOW

1. What happens when you die

When you die, your affairs need to be sorted out by someone. Debts need to be paid, accounts closed, assets sold – there's a lot to do.

Most people know that they should have a will in place before they die. A will is an instruction document nominating your **executors** (the person or people who sort everything out for you) and instructing them about what you want to happen. But although most of us know this is good practice, nearly 60% of people don't have a written will in place, according to a 2016 study by Unbiased.co.uk.[8]

If you die without a will, you are said to have died **intestate**. In that case, what happens after you die is decided by the **laws of intestacy**. In other words, the government decides. It's a mistake to think that your partner will get everything if you haven't made a will. It depends very much on what you own and how much it is worth.

Let's not beat around the bush here. If you have not made a will yet, this is your absolute number one priority right now. Stop reading this and do a search for local solicitors or will-writers near you. Make an appointment and get this sorted. They will be able to advise you about the terms of your will and help you come up with something which works for you. A few days from now, you could have a will in place – a great outcome. Just make sure to read the rest of this chapter before your appointment!

Of course, I know why people put off making a will. It isn't a fun thing to do, and requires us to think about our own death and what might happen to those left behind. But mature adults are intentional about sorting out their finances. That's why you're reading this book.

---

8   business.unbiased.co.uk/press-releases/fewer-people-in-the-uk-have-wills-in-place-than-last-year-with-nearly-four-in-ten-over-55s-having-no-will-at-all-26-9-2016

It doesn't matter how old you are. If you're an adult and have any kind of financial arrangements in place, you should have a will. Most wills can be very simple and hence do not need to be expensive.

2. What is included in a will

Before you make a will, you need to think about a few things, so that they can be properly addressed when your will is written.

⇨ **Executors** – who will sort everything out for you when you die? This is a big responsibility, so choose wisely. Usually, people opt for a close family member or two – people they trust. Or you can choose a professional executor, like the solicitor who wrote the will for you.

⇨ **Funeral wishes** – here's where you give instructions about whether you want to be buried, cremated or something else, and whether you want a religious funeral or not. Whatever you want to happen with your remains, this is where you let your executors know.

⇨ **Specific gifts** – if you want to make specific gifts to certain people, these are usually dealt with first. You might want to leave your valuable collection of Star Wars figures to your nephew Jonny, who would appreciate them, rather than have them sold and the money distributed. Or you might want to give your favourite podcast host £10,000 for all the value he has given over the years.

⇨ **Your residual estate** – this is what's left after the specific gifts have been sorted out and you need to decide here who gets what proportion. Usually, everything is sold, any debts paid, and then whatever is left is distributed according to your instructions here.

⇨ **Guardianship** – if you have children you should give some thought as to who would raise the kids for you. Make sure to talk to your prospective guardians first, as it is obviously a huge responsibility for them to take on. Also, you should provide some finance in your insurance programme so that if the worst happens, the guardians don't have to bear the full financial burden of your request.

It is so important to think this stuff through carefully. If you're in a couple, talk about it sensibly and gently, without seeking to impose your own views on the other party. Work together to come to an agreement about what happens when you die. Again, a good solicitor or will writer can advise you.

3. Power of attorney

While a will is a document for what you would want to happen after you die, a power of attorney gives instructions about what you would want to happen if you're still alive, but no longer have the capacity to make decisions for yourself.

Think about it. If you are in a car accident and end up in a coma, your bills and mortgage still need to be paid. Your bank account still needs to be managed, and someone will need to talk to your boss about whether and when you might return to work.

Most people understandably don't give this a moment's thought. They just assume that it will all be OK, somehow. In the UK, we have the Court of Protection that will assign someone to act on your behalf, called a deputy, if you cannot manage your own affairs. Applying to the court can be a slow process, and you must ask yourself if you are happy for someone you don't know to be responsible for sorting everything out for you. Far better to have thought about this in advance and put your own measures in place.

A lasting power of attorney, or LPA, can come in two flavours. The first is a **health and welfare LPA**, which gives your chosen attorneys the power to make decisions about your medical care and welfare if you can no longer do so for yourself. This might extend as far as making a decision to turn off life support, or about which care home you end up in – big decisions indeed.

The other type is a **property and financial LPA**, which, as the name suggests, gives your attorneys authority to deal with all your financial affairs if you can no longer do so.

When your attorney presents a valid LPA to your bank, the bank sees it as dealing directly with you, just through an authorised third party. They will want to see the original LPA document, which will have been ratified by the court. Only then will they talk to your attorney and provide details and access to your bank accounts.

There are limits to what your attorneys can do. They cannot, for example, award themselves huge gifts out of your money. Nor can they give your money away to other people, other than small amounts that you may reasonably be expected to give away for things like birthdays and Christmas.

An attorney's job is to manage your affairs for your benefit, as you would yourself. They are very tightly controlled by the court and there are severe punishments for attorneys who breach the trust given to them.

4. Trusts

The last mechanism you need to understand for organising things effectively, both after you have gone and while you're still around, is a trust.

Think of a trust as a box, into which you put some kind of asset. It might be a house, an investment or the proceeds of a life insurance policy or pension. The money or asset goes into the box and is managed according to the terms of the trust. There are three parties involved in this process:

1. **Settlor** – the person setting up the trust.

2. **Trustee** – the person or people entrusted by the settlor to look after the assets inside the trust.

3. **Beneficiaries** – the person or people who will eventually receive the assets in the trust.

Trusts are generally used for handling specific instructions for specific assets. You will have heard of a trust fund, which conjures up images of the children of billionaires whose every whim is provided for by a pot of money stashed away for them by mummy and daddy.

For most of us, reality is more mundane. One frequent use of trusts is for life insurance policies.

Let's say you have nominated your brother and sister-in-law to be guardians of your five-year-old daughter if you die, and you want to provide some money for them to help them raise the child. You might take out a life insurance policy and place that policy in trust.

In this case, you would be the **settlor**, putting the policy in trust. Your brother and sister-in-law would be the **beneficiaries** of the trust – the money would pay out to them. You would also be the **trustee**, making sure the life insurance policy is kept up to date, but you should also nominate another trustee, perhaps your brother, who would put in the life insurance claim if you were to die and make sure it pays out quickly.

Another example might be providing life insurance cover specifically for your daughter. Again, you would take out life insurance and place it into trust and you would be both settlor and trustee. You should also nominate your brother as a second trustee to deal with things if you die. Your daughter would be the beneficiary.

But let's say you die when your daughter is only eight years old. As she is still a child, she cannot legally receive the proceeds of the trust. Instead, the life insurance policy would pay out, and the money would go into a bank account in the trustee's name. His job would be to look after the money until your daughter reaches age 18, at which point she can access the money in her own right.

There are very strict rules about what trustees can do with the money they are entrusted with. For money which needs looking after for the long term, there are also requirements about how it should be managed and invested for the beneficiaries' best interest. Being a trustee is an onerous responsibility, so you need to choose wisely.

Everything you need to DO

1. Write a will

You got the message in the previous section, I'm sure, but it is hard to overstate the importance of making a will. Every adult should have one, without exception.

I urge you to get this done professionally. Yes, you will pay for it, and yes, you can go to a stationery shop and get a DIY will pack for next to nothing. Hopefully I've impressed on you just how important this is, and that getting it wrong is almost as bad as not making a will at all.

A good professionally written will gives you peace of mind while you're alive and makes life easier for your loved ones when you have gone. It's hard to put a price on that, but it certainly means that the cost of getting a will done right is worth every penny.

Check out the Law Society website[9] or the Society of Will Writers[10] to find a will-writing professional near you.

Before you instruct someone to write a will for you:

1. **Decide what you want to happen.** Talk to your partner if you have one and come up with an agreed strategy regarding all your assets, and what you would want to happen if one of you died, or if you both died together. Decide what specific gifts you might want to make and then agree the distribution of what's left.

2. **Calculate your worth.** Add up the value of everything you own and take off the balance of what you owe. Do this individually and as a couple. Itemise the major things like houses, cars, key items of furniture or art, to make it easy for the will-writer to take these into account.

3. **Decide on guardians and approach them.** Get the prospective guardian's permission to include them in your will.

---

9   solicitors.lawsociety.org.uk
10 www.willwriters.com/members

4. **Decide on your funeral wishes**. Choose your hymns, poems, or favourite rock music for the funeral and what you want to happen with your body.

5. **Decide on your executors and approach them**. Choose trusted friends or family members. In the absence of these, you can choose a professional trustee, usually a solicitor.

2. Arrange powers of attorney

It sounds like powers of attorney should only be prepared by old people who have a greater prospect of suffering from dementia, but everyone should have a power of attorney. In my career, I have had to help family members sort out the mess left when a much younger person has been involved in an accident or had a stroke.

The simplest way to do this is to nominate your partner as your attorney and vice versa. If you're single, ask a close friend or family member to act for you. Choose your attorneys wisely and consider having multiple attorneys. This relieves the burden from just one person and provides some accountability between the attorneys as well as to the Court of Protection. Make sure the two attorneys get along – they may need to work closely together for your benefit.

The same solicitor or will-writer who wrote your will can also arrange your lasting powers of attorney. You should ask for a discount if you're getting everything done together.

3. Place life insurance in trust

In almost every case, it makes sense to either write life insurance policies on a **life of another** basis, or to place them into trust. The main reason for this is to enable the proceeds of the policy to be paid out quickly to those who need it.

When a life insurance policy is owned by the person who has died, the proceeds form part of their estate. The executors will need to collect the money, complete the process of applying for probate and eventually pay the money out to the beneficiaries of the will. This process can take months and sometimes longer.

One other consideration can be inheritance tax, which I deal with in a later chapter. For now, you just need to understand that if the value of your estate is over a certain level, there may be tax to pay before any part of your estate can be paid out to the beneficiaries. It makes no sense to pay premiums into a life insurance policy for years, only to have a chunk of the policy proceeds taken away to pay a tax bill.

Placing the policy in trust avoids this issue and makes sure that the proceeds of the policy are ring-fenced for the benefit of those you intend. Most life insurance companies provide trust deeds which you can fill in yourself, or an adviser can help you to do this.

4. Nominate beneficiaries on pensions

We haven't even covered pensions yet – that's coming in the next section – but while you're thinking about what happens after death, you need to include benefits from your pension and employer.

There are lots of different kinds of pensions, but nearly all of them will provide some kind of death benefit for after you've gone. That's especially true if you have a spouse or partner who is dependent on you. This benefit might be a reduced pension, or alternatively the full value of the fund could be paid out. In each case you need to tell the pension company who you would like those benefits paid out to.

Approach all your pension companies, including previous employers, and find out what the benefits would be in the event of your death. Ask for the forms for nominating who those benefits should be paid out to and make sure you complete them urgently.

Ask the human resources department of your employer about death-in-service benefit, which is a life insurance policy provided by your company. If there is such a scheme, you will also have the chance to nominate who should benefit.

Death in service benefits and many pension benefits are held in a kind of master trust arrangement and don't normally form part of your estate. Make sure you understand what the arrangements are for all your work and pension benefits and tidy them up so that they get paid to the right people at the right time. Add these benefits to your one-page summary.

OK. Let's look at what you should now have in hand after taking action on this section of the book. You should have:

⇨ Understood the three main risks to your financial future and the different kinds of insurance designed to deal with each.

⇨ Assessed the impact each of the events might have on your immediate financial situation, and worked out how much insurance is needed to cover yourself and your family.

⇨ Applied for the insurance you need and made a good record of what you have taken out to be able to refer to it later.

⇨ Decided on what you want to happen after you die or if you cannot make your own decisions, and begun the process of making or reviewing your will and taking out a power of attorney.

This section is a little depressing, I know. It focuses on what might happen to you and your financial future if something bad happens to you or your family.

But it is **so** important to lay the foundation of a good insurance programme before you start building for your future, so please make sure you take the action detailed in each chapter. I'm telling you, the peace of mind you will gain from having this stuff in place is immeasurable.

Probably fewer than one in 100 people have this stuff done right. That could be you and your family would thank you if it was.

But now let's turn our minds to building a financial future on top of this firm foundation we have laid. Let's talk about making money!

Step 3

Invest Wisely

LET'S NOT BEAT AROUND THE bush here – this is the fun part!

Financial success comes from repeating a few simple actions over and over again for the long haul. Sure, you might win the lottery, receive a big inheritance or trip over the neighbour's dog and win a compensation claim. But you also might not, and in that case, you'd better have a Plan A.

Now that you have mastery of your monthly budget, and you have a sure foundation of insurance against the worst life can throw at you, it's time to begin laying brick upon brick to build a financial future that you can enjoy both now and in the years ahead.

It can be so tempting to jump ahead and dive into the making money part of the plan, but remember the guy who built his house on the sand – when things went wrong, they went really wrong. If you haven't fully absorbed and implemented the lessons of Steps One and Two, I strongly urge you to do so now.

Looking ahead, in this section I cover the important difference between saving and investing, and teach you about the essential link between risk, timescale and the rewards you can enjoy by investing.

Then we look at the building blocks of an investment portfolio and how they all fit together. By the way, a *portfolio* is just a fancy word for your investments when viewed as a whole. Plus it sounds good when you talk to your friends about your portfolio. Try it – you'll feel like the Wolf of Wall Street.

There's no way we can talk about investing without going over the basics of tax and how to make use of all the valuable tax allowances available to you. And then finally I give you the very practical steps you need to begin building an investment strategy that will help you achieve your life goals.

I'm excited – are you? *Then let's get going.*

Chapter 12
Saving and Investing

SAVING AND INVESTING (I EXPLAIN the difference shortly) is a future-focused activity. You will see the results of your actions in the years and decades ahead. Because this is the case, it is important to have a plan for what you're doing, so you understand where you are now, where you're heading, and so you have a route to get from here to there.

Any great building starts off as a plan on a sheet of paper, or more likely, a CAD document on a computer somewhere. If the first thing that happened in the development of any building project was that someone turned up with a machine and started digging foundations, how would they end up in the right place? No one would even know what the right place was and the building would never make it out of the ground.

Likewise, your financial future requires some thought before you take action. It isn't possible for most people to fully visualise what their retirement will look like, but the next five years are much easier to consider. Longer-term investing is pretty much a 'save as much as you can' deal, but as your goals come closer, you can refine your approach accordingly.

We begin by looking at the basics of saving, investing and setting goals in this chapter, before steadily adding detail over the coming chapters.

Everything you need to KNOW

1. Saving versus investing

For most people, the difference between saving and investing is semantics, just different words for the same thing. I draw some important distinctions between the two, as follows.

Saving is short term, investing is long term

When you **save** money, it is likely to be used in the next three years, for things like Christmas, next year's holiday, or your anniversary the year after next.

When you **invest**, it is towards things which are more than four or five years into the future. Things like your kids' private education or university costs, your daughter's wedding one day, or the big one: your retirement.

Saving is done by putting money in the bank, investing involves buying assets

Saving involves moving money in the form of cash from your main current account into a separate savings account.

Investing, by contrast, involves using your money in the bank to buy other kinds of asset, such as property, shares, or even gold. Investment professionals refer to different kinds of things you can invest in as *asset classes*, but don't be deterred by this jargon.

When saving, you earn interest, when investing you get 'total return'

Money held in the bank will earn interest. It's the bank's way of paying you for letting them use your money for their other projects, like lending to mortgage borrowers.

If you buy assets, you usually get two strings to your bow. You can earn an income in the form of interest or dividends, or if you own property, your income is rent. You can also benefit from the assets you bought rising in value. The combination of the two is called total return. You'll often hear 'total return' shortened to just 'return' or 'returns'.

Saving will not produce wealth, investing for the long term will

Keeping your cash in the bank, as we'll see in Chapters 12 and 13 , is no way to build wealth. In the ten years up to this book being published, interest rates in the UK have been 0.5% per year or even lower. For almost all of those ten years, inflation has been higher than 0.5%. This means that money saved in the bank is actually losing value, thanks to the impact of inflation.

Money which is invested, on the other hand, tends to increase in value over time. It doesn't always happen in a straight line, as we shall see, but usually investments comfortably outperform inflation over the long run, so the value of your money increases.

Saving is risk-free, investing involves some risk

Cash in the bank is generally considered risk-free. Deposits in banks in the UK are insured by the government under the Financial Services Compensation Scheme (FSCS), up to £85,000 per person, per bank. Even if your bank fails and your money is lost, the government would step in and pay you the money back, up to that level.

Investments come with all kinds of risks, as we shall see in the next chapter. Far from being a bad thing, risk is part of the engine of wealth-building.

Saving has no explicit cost, investing has costs

Most banks don't charge you for depositing your money with them, though some banks do charge for current accounts which are enhanced with benefits like travel insurance.

Investing involves various levels of charges. There are transaction costs, platform and wrapper costs, taxation and sometimes advice costs.

Needless to say, in order to offset these costs, you hope to do better by investing than you would by leaving your money saved in the bank.

Saving is rate-driven, investing requires knowledge and education

When deciding where to save your money, the best choice is likely to be the bank offering you the highest rate of interest. These days you can compare hundreds of bank accounts easily using comparison websites. One bank is much the same as another and as long as the FSCS protection applies, you might as well shop around for the best deal.

When it comes to choosing investments, there are many other factors at play, such as the past performance of your chosen shares or funds, the state and outlook of the world economy, the ease with which you can take your money out, and more factors besides. Because of this, you need to do a bit more homework than spending five minutes on a comparison site.

2. Cash is not an investment

Investing has the potential to help you grow your money over the long term, but the perceived complexity is why so many people never really get started. Don't worry though. Over the next few chapters, I will give you all the information you need to set up an investment programme that will help you meet your goals.

For now, repeat this mantra after me (regular listeners to my podcast will already know this):

Cash is NOT an investment.

Say it again:

Cash is NOT an investment.

No one builds wealth effectively in the early 21st century by keeping money in cash. By the way, I don't mean literal bank notes under your mattress, but holding your money in low-interest bank accounts.

You should only keep enough cash in the bank to cover any emergencies such as losing your job or having a major repair bill to pay, and short-term savings. Remember the emergency fund discussed earlier? Any money on top of that should be put to better use by investing it.

Got that? Excellent – let's move on.

3. All saving and investing should be done with an end in mind

When a new prospective client approaches me because they have some money to invest, my first question back to them will always be 'why?'. If there's no 'why,' there's no possible way I can determine what the best approach might be for them.

Depending on how far forward we are looking, the 'why' may be more or less distinct, but there still needs to be something on the horizon that you're moving towards.

If ever I get the sense that the only reason someone wants me to help them invest is 'to get richer' then I'm not interested. The joy of investing money is to work towards a given end: a secure retirement, a dream holiday or the classic car you've always wanted. These things make people happy; zeroes on a bank statement do not.

In my experience, people who are just seeking wealth for its own sake are generally unpleasant folks who are never happy with anything. If they get a 10% annual return they complain they didn't get 15%, and they're always comparing the size and performance of their portfolio with their friends and colleagues.

But that's not you. Instead, you're going to start dreaming of what you want to work towards.

Everything you need to DO

1. Create goals

Anyone who has worked in a business environment will have heard of SMART goals. The SMART acronym stands for Specific, Measureable, Achievable, Relevant and Time-bound. The thinking is that unless a goal has all these attributes, then it isn't a goal at all.

I happen to think that SMART is a bit wordy, and we can probably distil things down to just M and T. In other words, they should be measurable and have a timescale.

When thinking about financial goals, the measurable part usually pertains to the amount of money, either in capital or income, that you will need to do whatever it is you want to do. The timescale is self-explanatory – when will you want to have achieved your goal by?

Sit down, together if you're in a relationship, and dream a little. What would you like to have happen in life? Do you plan to have kids? If so, when? What would a perfect year look like? How many holidays? Would you want to work full- or part-time?

Would you like to buy a house one day? If so, where would you live and what kind of house would it be? How many bedrooms? Would it be a house in the country or a penthouse apartment in the city?

Then think a little bit longer term. If you have kids, would you like them to be educated privately, or would you like to be able to support them through university? Would you like to help them onto the housing ladder or be able to pay for the wedding of their dreams?

Then think about the end goal. What are you working towards? Do you plan to retire one day? If so, what would that look like? Would it really be about doing nothing all day and watching daytime TV, or would it involve some volunteer work, or worldwide travel, or starting your own business on your own terms?

All the above are fairly generic goals, but the great thing here is that your goals will be uniquely yours. You get to design your life how you want it. Of course, you may not be able to achieve everything you desire. If your goal is to fly on your private jet to the Maldives for three months of the year, then alternate between apartments in London and New York, dining in Michelin starred restaurants and driving the best cars, but you're currently a shift manager in McDonalds, then you may need to set your sights a little lower.

That said, we live in a world of unprecedented opportunity. The internet means we are more connected than ever before, and that presents more opportunity for you to build a business than was even remotely possible just 20 years ago. I follow people online with seven-figure businesses operating from their home, all online. There is a far greater chance of you realising your globe-trotting dreams in 2018 than there was in 1998 if you're prepared to do the work and maybe get a little bit lucky.

Assuming you will follow a career path in your chosen profession, and can expect steadily increasing wages, then your financial success will be down to your implementing the three steps to financial success every day, week, month and year. But in so doing, you have the capacity to amass as much wealth as you could possibly need.

2. Try to put a price on your goals

The only way to do this effectively is to think in today's money. By that I mean, when coming up with a price for, say, a dream holiday in five years' time, you need to price up that holiday based on what it would cost today. (You may be wondering about inflation – ignore that for now, we'll deal with it shortly.)

If you were to buy your dream home now, what would it cost? If you were to take that cruise this summer, how much would you pay? If you want to send one child to private school from age 11, what are the fees for each term? Is there a discount for two kids?

It's fairly easy to research these things as the costs are freely available on websites and in brochures. But it is more difficult to put a price on something very far off and somewhat intangible, like retirement.

When thinking about setting retirement goals, if it is more than ten years into the future, I wouldn't waste too much time trying to be too exact. Instead, think about how much it might cost on an annual or monthly basis, to sustain a nice lifestyle now, if you weren't working. This is simply a case of working out your monthly outgoings, maybe taking off your mortgage as you will hopefully have paid that off by the time you retire, taking off any life insurance costs or savings and then adding back any nice-to-have things. These might involve changing the car every few years or having two holidays each year. Remember, it's your retirement.

Set your goal to the nearest £250 or £500 per month and that'll do for now.

Our goals and plans tend to get more refined the nearer we get to achieving them. Those goals that are next year or two years out are the most distinct. Five-year goals are a little woollier, and for most of us, retirement is an indistinct glowing blob way into the future somewhere.

This is the reason why most people seek financial advice. Most people can do perfectly well meeting short- and medium-term goals, but when it comes to planning their retirement, they need help, because that blob won't stay indistinct forever. It comes ever more into focus and as we get into our late forties, fifties and sixties, it starts to come very clearly into view.

I suggest that you write down a handful of goals in the following format:

"I would like to have saved £X by such and such a date, to enable me to do Y."

Yours might look like this:

"I would like to have saved £5,000 by next summer so that we can enjoy a family holiday without putting it on the credit card."

or:

"I would like to retire at age 60, and enjoy a £2,000 per month lifestyle."

Make sure there's an amount and a timescale. This is important because it will help you determine how to invest your money to reach your goals.

Chapter 13
Risk, Timescale and Reward

WAIT, WHAT? RISK? I DON'T like the sound of that!

It's time to become familiar with risk because it is an unavoidable part of successful investing. In fact you wouldn't want to avoid it, as risk is actually a tool that you can use when investing to give yourself the best chance of meeting your goals.

Everything you need to KNOW

1. Risk comes in different forms

When it comes to saving and investing, there are quite a few different risks you need to be aware of, and some of them may not be as you might think.

Inflation risk

Inflation is the word used to describe the general increase in prices over time. Ask your parents how much they bought their first house for, and you'll see inflation at work. My parents bought the house I was raised in for about £4,000 in 1980. I paid twice that for my little car, and 45 times that for the house I have raised my own kids in. That's inflation – generally, the cost of things goes up.

In some cases it doesn't. I'm looking at my iPhone right now; its processing power would have cost millions in 1980, if it was available at all. In that case, the cost of one unit of computing power has reduced significantly.

For the most part though, inflation means that prices rise. When I talk about inflation as a risk, I mean that risk works against you as an investor.

The purpose of investing is to make your money grow. You want to turn £100 into £200 so that you can buy something with it. You invest in such a way that you can expect the £100 to grow to £200 in five years. The problem is, when you get to five years' time, the thing that did cost £200 now costs £250, so you have to work a little bit harder.

To put it another way, if costs rise by, say, 3% every year and your investments grow by 7%, then actually, the buying power of your money has only grown by 4%. Inflation has swallowed up 3% of the growth.

In recent years, inflation has been fairly predictable in the UK. It seems like the bad old days of double-digit inflation are banished to the past, which is a good thing, but inflation will always be a part of life, so we need to understand and embrace it.

Inertia risk

This is the risk of missing out by doing nothing. Everything I'm going to teach over the next few chapters works, I promise you that, but only if you take action.

Too many people wait too long to get going because they're scared they'll mess things up, or they just want to read one more book before they start investing.

One of the mantras of successful investing is that the length of time you are invested is more important than many other factors and variables, including trying to start at some kind of optimum point. The best thing you can do is to start now. The longer you're invested, the more time you have to grow your money, so why wait?

Inertia is the opposite of being intentional. It is dithering and worrying when you should be acting and executing. That's not you, but be warned that it can always be a temptation – you're only human after all.

Longevity risk

This is one for the older folks looking to retire – the risk that you might outlive your money.

I spend a lot of my time at work helping people to plan their retirement so that they spend down their money over time, maybe leave some for the kids to inherit, and hopefully have enough to pay for care if they need it in their final years.

The worst-case scenario for these people is that they might reach age 80, still be in excellent health, and then run out of money and have to sell their house or make radical changes to their lifestyle. People tend to underestimate their longevity, but the average 65-year-old will live about 20 years, which I'm sure you'll agree is a very long time to go without earning a living.

Imagine if you decided to take a 20-year holiday starting tomorrow. How soon would your money run out? That's why it is important firstly to make provision by saving hard for retirement, but also to plan the process of spending that money when the time comes.

Investment risk

This is what most people think of when they think about investing. Primarily this means the risk that you buy something with your cash in the hope that its value will rise, but instead it drops in value and you lose money.

It can also mean the risk that the bank, insurance company or investment provider to whom you entrust your money goes bust and you lose everything. Fortunately this is very rare and there are certain protections available to you under the UK's Financial Services Compensation Scheme.

Some investments are riskier than others. By this, I mean that the value of the asset fluctuates more widely over time. Take a look at the chart below. You can see that while both lines head upwards over time, the dark line goes up and down in value far more than the lighter line, which is much smoother. This is how to think about the risk of different investments – how wobbly that line is. We refer to the wobbliness of the line as the volatility of the investment. As we'll learn, you can use this wobbliness or volatility to your advantage in building wealth.

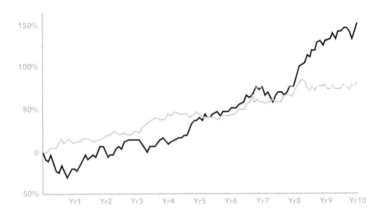

Behaviour risk

No matter how volatile an investment is (how wobbly the line is), you will only ever lose money if you sell the asset for less than you bought it for. If you don't sell it, it may be valued lower than you would like at a given point in time, but until you realise the asset, that is, convert it back into cash by selling it, you haven't really lost anything.

Of course, this is easy to say, but difficult to experience in practice. It isn't fun to receive a statement from your investment company one year and see that the value is lower than it was last year. If that happens two or three years in a row, then you may well be tempted to bail out. But that's the point at which you lose money.

The way we behave around money is perhaps the biggest risk of all. That's why it is important to understand how money works so that we can try to make decisions which are informed, rather than over-emotional.

2. Risk and reward are linked

There is an undisputable link between the level of risk you are prepared to take and the returns you can expect to receive. Let's take this to extremes in an example.

Two people receive a £100,000 inheritance. John puts the money in a bank account with an interest rate of 1% and spends the £1,000 interest every year until he dies. His beneficiaries will receive the £100,000 in full because all John has spent is the interest, not the capital.

Jane on the other hand takes her £100,000 inheritance to Kempton Park racecourse where she bets it all on the outside chance horse in the race at 3:30pm.

In Scenario A, Jane wins at 500:1 odds and pockets £5 million in winnings, plus she gets her stake back – not a bad afternoon's work.

In Scenario B, Jane's horse falls in the first furlong and she loses everything.

John's wealth will never increase because he spends his £1000 interest each year, but at least he won't lose anything by keeping the money in the bank. Jane can either win big or lose the lot.

The point is that Jane **could** get a massive return on her money because she is prepared to risk it. John is not prepared to take that risk and is satisfied that he will receive a fairly uninspiring level of interest as a result.

Fortunately, investing is much more nuanced than betting on horses and it is possible to build a portfolio with an anticipated level of return and a relatively predictable level of risk.

For now, though, you just need to accept the link between risk and reward. We'll put some flesh on the bones of that when we talk about the different things in which you can invest in the next chapter.

3. Risk tolerance and capacity for loss

It is one thing to talk about the risk of a particular kind of investment, but it's quite another to talk about how **you** might react when your money is invested and the value of it is going up and down.

Think about it. You work hard to get together £10,000 to invest. You do so and when you log in to your account three weeks later, you see that the value has dropped to £9,500 – how do you feel? What about if the value had dropped to £8,000? Or £5,000? Or if it had risen to £12,000?

Your ability to cope emotionally with the inherent volatility of investments is called your attitude to risk, or your **risk tolerance**.

There are many factors which have shaped you into the human being you are today. The way your parents talked about money in front of you, the early experiences you had when financially independent for the first time; these influences and more all form part of your unique money story. Your relationship with money and your attitude towards abstract concepts like investment risk are all informed by this money story.

Your **capacity for loss** is different. This term refers to your financial ability to withstand the loss of your money.

If your £10,000 investment represents all the money you have in the world, your capacity for losing that money is much lower than the next person, who happens to be worth £10 million. If you lose your money it would be disastrous. If the other woman loses £10,000 out of her £10 million portfolio, she'll barely notice.

Both risk tolerance and capacity for loss are important considerations when building any portfolio of investments. They will inform the level of risk you should take.

4. Risk can be managed

Within reason, it is possible to manage the risk of any investment in three main ways:

1. **Diversification** – this is a fancy word for spreading your money around. You've heard the expression that you shouldn't put all your eggs in one basket? Diversification is the practical application of that when it comes to investments. You should have different kinds of account and your investment portfolio should be made up of different kinds of investment assets. Each of these represents a different basket into which you place your money eggs.

2. **Time** – it has long been proven that the returns of any portfolio become more predictable the longer you hold it. A moderately adventurous portfolio, for example, might return 7% per year on average over ten years. In any one year, it could go up 25%, or drop by 15% or even more. The longer you hold the investment, the more the range of likely returns reverts to the average of 7% per year. I'll unpack this a little more later, but for now, take it from me that holding investments for longer effectively reduces the risk.

3. **Review** – an investment that is ignored over time is in danger of drifting far from its original intention, therefore it is good practice to review your investments regularly. That doesn't necessarily mean that you will need to change them, but rather that you should keep an eye on them. There is an anecdotal story from the US where a major investment company analysed the best performing accounts over a given time period. When they approached the people who owned those accounts, most of them had forgotten they even had an account with the investment company! As we'll see later on, unnecessary tinkering with your portfolio can do more harm than good, but forgetting about it altogether isn't really the approach of someone who is intentional about their wealth-building.

Fortunately, it is easy to build these three risk-management approaches into your plan, as we'll see.

5. Investment returns versus investor returns – the behaviour gap

The story about forgetful investors with well-performing accounts is a good parable for talking about **the behaviour gap**. I'm not sure who coined the phrase originally, but it has certainly been made famous by US-based financial adviser Carl Richards,[11] who has a fantastic ability to explain complex concepts using simple diagrams.

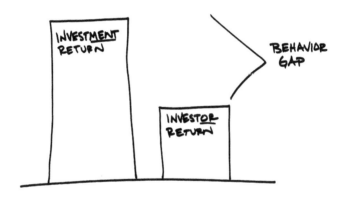

As shown in the diagram, the distance between the return of an asset and the return earned by investors in that asset is the behaviour gap.

Investments perform based on the laws of supply and demand, and based on sentiment – how the market feels about the particular

---

11   www.behaviorgap.com

investment. The value of investments will go up and down over time, but generally, the trend is up.

The problem is that people get in the way. They try to invest at *just the right time*. They fiddle with their portfolios and incur costs in doing so. They panic and sell out when they should be putting more money in. In short, humans are not the brightest when it comes to investing.

Benjamin Graham, the so-called father of value investing and author of *The Intelligent Investor*, coined this phrase:

> "The investor's chief problem, and even his worst enemy, is likely to be himself."

I have that quote in huge letters on my office wall, so clients are constantly reminded of it.

A key risk you need to be aware of is your own tendency to sabotage your investment returns.

Everything you need to DO

That was a pretty meaty KNOW section, so let's get to a couple of practical steps you can take to implement what we know about risk, timescale and reward.

1. Get your attitude to risk assessed

If you instruct an adviser to help you with your financial planning, they will take you through a risk tolerance measurement process. If you want to do this yourself, the best place I know is at meaningfulmoney. tv/myrisktolerance.

The smart people who developed this risk tool have used lots of academic research to create and maintain it. You will pay about £30 per person for the assessment, but in the grand scheme of things it is a small price to pay, as the output will be useful in helping you get going with your investing.

The end result is a report showing your risk profile compared with the population as a whole, based on your answers. There is also detail about how someone in your tolerance bracket might respond to market events and how they view risk as a whole.

A Google search may throw up some free ways of assessing your risk tolerance, but be wary, as not all risk questionnaires are created equal. Some are linked to specific products and can steer you in a certain direction. Others have questions which are unnecessarily leading in nature.

Whichever risk profile tool you use, you will probably fall into one of three broad categories:

1. **Cautious** – You are concerned that you might lose money, but you understand that some risk is necessary to build wealth. You don't enjoy watching your money rise and fall in value, and if it gets too bad, you might be tempted to bail out.

2. **Balanced** – You are happy with some risk and understand that investments rise and fall, sometimes considerably. You might get nervous with large market movements, but generally you should be able to hang in there for the long haul.

3. **Adventurous** – You're very comfortable with the ups and downs that investments undergo, and don't worry very much about it. You certainly don't lose any sleep worrying about your money because you know that in the long run, it'll be OK.

There are lots of nuances to this, of course, and as many interpretations as there are people on earth. You may see modifiers applied to the terms above, such as Moderately Cautious or Balanced Plus. Each profiling system is different and it is always important to read the output to see if it does indeed reflect your feelings about investing.

Finally, remember that if you're new to investing, you don't have much of a frame of reference for risk tolerance. In this case, you should probably err towards caution.

2. Consider using different pots for different goals

Not too long ago, people often saved money in cash pots, using old jam jars or the like. They maybe had one pot for birthdays, another for Christmas and another for next year's trip to the seaside.

The same paradigm can still work today, even if the physical jam jars have been replaced with online saving and investment accounts.

If you have different things you are saving for, with differing timescales to meet them, consider using different accounts to keep the money separate. It'll keep your mind clear and you'll be able to keep track of things easily.

I have a separate bank account into which we put an amount every month for Christmas. We have another bank account into which we save for bigger things like holidays and changing the car. Then we have investment ISAs for things like the girls' university fund. And of course, we have pensions for retirement.

With the proliferation of online investment platforms and online banking, it is so easy to set up virtual pots for your different financial goals, to move money between them, and to stay on top of them over time.

3. Remember – a loss is only a loss when you realise it

Ok, so this is more of a KNOW than a DO, but I wanted to put it right at the end of the chapter so it would resonate strongly.

Let's say you invest £10,000 and, one year later, you get a statement and it shows the pot is worth £12,000 – how do you feel?

The following year, your statement says the value is £8,000. You've lost £4,000! How do you feel then?

Of course, you haven't lost anything yet. It's just that the value of your investments has changed. If you don't need to spend that money in the near future, you could let it run and hopefully it will regain its former value. Or you could sell the investment in a rash panic, in case it gets any worse.

This is why you should never invest money you might need in the short term. You must be able to give any investment time to work, to ride out the ups and downs.

The best piece of risk-management advice I can give you is to understand that until you sell your investments and receive the cash for them back into your bank account, the value of them is largely theoretical.

This means that you do not need to get too hung up the values on your investment statements as you move towards your goals. Yes, you'll need to review things now and then, but you must not panic based on a number at a single point on the journey. Remember the behaviour gap – don't be your own worst enemy.

Chapter 14
Asset Classes

INVESTING HAPPENS ACROSS A FEW different levels. The next few chapters will address each of the four main levels in turn. In short, they are:

1. **Asset** – This is the most granular level and represents the underlying investments you hold. Assets are what you buy with your money. Property is an asset, and so are shares and gold. I'll deal with the main asset classes you need to know about in this chapter.

2. **Fund** – Most people hold their assets within funds. This system, called collective investment, means you can pool your money together with many others and in doing so, you can reduce risk by spreading the money further and benefit from reduced costs. I look at this in Chapter 15.

3. **Wrapper** – A wrapper is a kind of box that you hold your assets within. An ISA is a wrapper, and so is a general investment account (GIA), and so is a pension, too. I look at wrappers in Chapter 16.

4. **Platform** – A platform is an online administration system where you can hold different kinds of wrappers under one roof. This makes it easy to move money around and organise your investments. You will find the detail about this in Chapter 17.

The diagram below shows how this works.

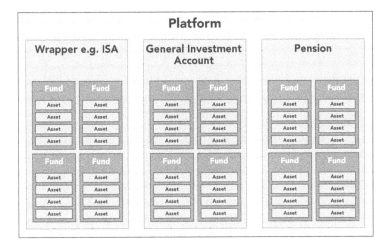

Everything you need to KNOW

1. The main asset classes

We group together assets into classes to make them easier to think about. Let me cover each of the main asset classes below and you'll see what I mean.

Cash

I know, I know. I said cash is not an investment. That's right, it isn't. But it does sometimes form part of a portfolio of other assets. Usually you hold some cash as part of a portfolio to pay fees, but generally, you wouldn't hold more than 1% or 2% of your **invested** money in cash. Remember, you have your emergency fund behind you, so you don't need to hold cash in your investment portfolio.

Bonds

The word *bond* is one of the most confusing words in personal finance to the layperson, because it means quite a few different things.

When banks offer fixed-term bank accounts, we sometimes call those three-year bonds or one-year bonds. There is a tax wrapper called an investment bond too, which I'll cover briefly in Chapter 16.

But really, a bond is an IOU. Let's say a big UK company like Marks & Spencer wants to open a new store. They can dip into their cash reserves or borrow money from a bank, or they can issue a bond, and ask ordinary investors like you and me to lend them the money to build the store.

In return for your money, you receive an IOU, which states the amount you have lent Marks & Spencer, the interest rate, called the **coupon**, which Marks & Spencer will pay you while they have your money, and the date at which Marks & Spencer will pay you back.

Your IOU might say something like:

> Marks & Spencer owes you £1000, which they will pay back on 1st July 2025, and they will pay you 3% coupon per year.

So far, so simple, but here's where it gets a bit more complex: these IOUs or bonds are traded on the stock market.

Imagine the trustees of a pension fund need a source of guaranteed income to pay out to their pensioners. They might want to buy the Marks & Spencer bond because they know it will pay out £30 per year (£1000 x 3%) guaranteed for the next few years, as long as the company doesn't go bust.

The pension trustees approach you and offer you £1100 for your bond. Congratulations, you have just made a £100 profit, because you paid £1000 for it. You pass the bond to the pension people and everyone is happy.

But hang on. In 2025 when Marks & Spencer pay back the money on the bond, now owned by the pension trustees, they will only pay back £1000, so the pension fund has lost £100 on the deal. That is the price they pay for securing that income. They have paid £100 to secure an income of £30 per year from the date at which they bought the bond off you until it is redeemed in 2025.

Millions of these bonds change hands every day on the world's stock markets. A bond has two main benefits. The first, its income stream, is by far the most important aspect. Secondly, the value of the bond, which is a function of both the income stream and the length of time left until it is redeemed.

Interest rates set by central banks can also have an impact on the value of bonds, as bonds become more or less attractive in light of the changing interest rate. If an investor can get a decent rate of interest from a bank account, why would they take the risk of investing in bonds?

One other thing you need to know about bonds is the quality scale.

As you can imagine, as a big company, Marks & Spencer does not have any difficulty in attracting investors for their bond offerings. They are a staple of the UK retail scene and though they have good times and bad, they are generally seen as a pretty safe bet, and pretty likely to pay back their IOUs.

Now let's say my company Jacksons Wealth issues a bond. We're a little financial advice firm in Penzance, and as such there's probably a larger chance that we might go bust than Marks & Spencer. So how might we attract investors to our bond offering?

The answer is by offering a higher coupon or interest rate. The quality scale of bonds is shown in the following diagram.

Bond Yield/Quality Scale

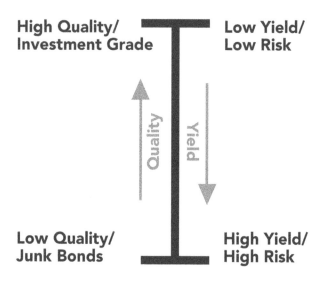

**High Quality/
Investment Grade**

**Low Yield/
Low Risk**

**Low Quality/
Junk Bonds**

**High Yield/
High Risk**

As you can see, the coupon, usually expressed as an interest rate percentage, is higher the lower down the quality scale you go. Sub-investment grade bonds, sometimes called junk bonds, offer the highest interest rates, but offer the biggest chance of loss. Investment-grade bonds are lower risk and hence offer a lower interest rate.

It's a little simplistic to say that bonds are lower risk than shares, though historically they have been less volatile and their returns a little smoother than shares. It is more accurate to say that bonds behave **differently** to shares, and that's why it's usually a good idea to hold some of each in any portfolio, to benefit from the returns of both kinds of investment.

When companies issue bonds they are called **corporate bonds**. When governments want to raise money, they can also issue bonds. In the UK, government-issued bonds are called **gilts**. In the US, they are called Treasury Bills, T-Bills or sometimes just Treasuries. Government bonds tend to be more secure than corporate bonds as they are backed by the government which issues them. Governments can go bust, but it doesn't tend to happen often and is less likely than a company going bust.

Finally, you may hear bonds as an asset class called *fixed interest* or *fixed income* investments. I think that's a little unhelpful, as these terms suggest fixed-rate bank accounts to me. But, as we have seen, the income is indeed fixed on a bond, even if its capital value is largely determined by the stock market.

Shares

A share is a tiny slice of a company. Usually when we invest in shares, we invest in listed companies whose shares are traded on the stock market. Shares are often also called **equities**.

Returns from shares come in two forms. Firstly, if the company makes a profit, a **dividend** may be issued, which is a distribution of the profit to the shareholders.

Secondly, the price of the share itself will **rise and fall** depending primarily on sentiment, in other words, what the market thinks about the company and its prospects. If the general feeling is that hard times are ahead, or that the company management isn't up to scratch, the share price may fall as there are likely to be more sellers than buyers.

If the company operates in a thriving market with good prospects and the management is top quality, then the share price may rise as more people will want to buy shares to take part in the company's success.

The ownership of a share gives you some rights. As well as receiving a dividend, you can vote on company decisions, though as a shareholder you would usually delegate the day-to-day running of the company to the board of directors, who are accountable to you and the other owners of the business.

Property

Property is a unique asset class. Almost everyone understands property because it is tangible. You can walk up to a property, stand inside it and run your hands along the walls. Many of us have paid rent in our lives too, so we understand that the owner of the property receives that rent and in return has to maintain the property to a good standard for the tenants.

Many people invest in property by buying physical buildings. Often, they borrow money in the form of a buy-to-let mortgage to do this. They have to make mortgage repayments of course, which reduces the net amount of rent they receive. In the last 20 years or so it has been easier than ever to get a buy-to-let mortgage, and according to HMRC figures from 2014, there are now 1.75 million private landlords in the UK.

An alternative way to invest in property is via a fund, where you pool your money with lots of other investors to buy big properties like car parks, shopping centres and shopping malls. More on this in the next chapter, but investing in this way gets around one of the biggest problems with investing in property.

That problem is that property can be **illiquid**. That's a lovely technical word (remember it though, it's important) which means that property can be difficult to sell. If you own an investment property and want to sell it, but the local housing market is sluggish, it may take months to sell your property, or you may have to sell for a reduced price. That could be a problem if you need the money quickly.

There are other issues to consider if you invest in physical property. If you have a mortgage, and for some reason you have a blank period, that is, a period of time where you don't have a tenant paying you rent, then you still have to pay the mortgage.

Landlords also have some serious responsibilities and duties under law. If they fail in any of these duties, they face prosecution, fines and even prison.

All that said, 1.75 million private landlords can't be wrong, and property remains one of the most popular asset classes in the UK, as the enduring popularity of The Property Podcast presented by my friends Rob Bence and Rob Dix attests.

Alternatives

The last major asset class sweeps up lots of smaller classes into one big lump, called alternatives. This might include:

⇨ **Commodities** – these are materials which we humans consume, like metals, oil and gas, and soft commodities like wheat, rice and orange juice.

⇨ **Gold** – as a metal, this strictly falls into the commodities category, but it has a special place in investors' hearts. The gold price is very volatile, but still many investors see gold as a safe-haven investment. It is seen this way because gold has historically performed well when share markets are falling or inflation is rising.

⇨ **Private equity** – this involves companies which buy up other companies or that invest in start-up firms. It's often racy stuff – be prepared to make or lose quite large amounts.

⇨ **Hedge funds** – hedge funds invest in such a way that they make money when stock markets are falling. They achieve this apparent miracle by borrowing shares from a third party and paying them a fee for doing so. They then sell the shares while the market is high and buy them back when the price has dropped. They pocket the difference and pass the shares back to the third party.

There are other asset classes which might fall into the alternatives group, but these are the main ones you might come across. Generally, the idea of alternatives is that they behave differently to the other classes. This comes in handy when you are trying to put together an investment portfolio.

2. The geography factor

As well as the different asset classes you can invest into, another consideration is the geographical location of your investments.

Let's say you decide to invest in shares. You could buy a portfolio of UK shares and be satisfied with your work. But what if I told you that the UK stock market only represents about 8% of the total value of the world stock markets. Wouldn't you want a slice of the 92% of value that lies outside the UK's shores? Wouldn't you want also to invest in the US, Europe, Japan or elsewhere?

Just as different assets classes behave differently, so do different geographical regions:

⇨ **Developed world** – these are the mostly Western, first-world economies such as the UK, USA and the eurozone, as well as some of the major Far Eastern economies like Japan. These are very highly developed and regulated markets, which are generally very liquid – easy to sell in and out of.

⇨ **Emerging markets** – these are countries which are aiming to catch up with the developed nations. Often they are very large economies, but with less developed markets and regulatory systems. Examples are Brazil, Russia, India and China. Emerging markets are generally more volatile than developed markets – you can make or lose a lot of money here.

⇨ **Frontier markets** – these are the next level down, including some of the African nations, and smaller Far Eastern countries like Vietnam. These are generally more volatile still than the emerging markets.

Wherever you invest, there are benefits and disadvantages of investing in that particular area. One factor which can either work for you or against you is **currency risk**.

Let's say you buy shares in an American company. You are a UK investor, so you have to convert your pounds into dollars. Let's say the exchange rate is $1.50 to £1.

You buy $1500 of shares and it costs you £1000 in sterling to do so. Good news, the share price increases by 10%, so now you have $1650 of shares in the company and you decide to call it quits.

You now need to bring your dollars back to the UK and exchange them into sterling. Unfortunately, the exchange rate has moved, and the exchange rate is now $1.65 for each £1 of sterling. Your $1650 equals £1000, which is exactly what you started with! All your profit has been wiped out by the change in the exchange rate.

There isn't much that ordinary investors can do to offset this risk. But the good thing is these currency moves should even out over time; sometimes they will be in your favour and sometimes against you, but over the long term they should not have a large impact in either direction.

3. Combining assets

Now we have learned about the different asset classes and geographical locations, we need to start putting some of this stuff together.

Investment professionals refer to this process of blending together different assets from around the world as *asset allocation*. But we don't need to worry about the technical terms. The idea is just to try and find a mix of assets that achieves a given level of return within acceptable levels of volatility or risk.

The risk part is managed by blending together assets which behave differently to one another. This produces a smoothing effect, so your investment returns are more predictable. Here's an example.

Let's say you hold shares in both an ice-cream company and an umbrella company. During a very hot, dry summer, the ice-cream company will do very well and its share price will rise. In the winter and spring the umbrella company will likely do better and its share price will rise.

If you just hold the ice-cream shares and it's a very wet, dreary summer your investment will suffer. If you hold only the umbrella shares and there is a drought lasting a few months, your investment will suffer.

By holding both, you get some benefit throughout the year, no matter what kind of weather you have.

In real life, the different assets always overlap a bit. It isn't as simple as when one asset class goes up, the other goes down; it is more nuanced than that.

Lower risk-tolerant investors usually hold a smaller allocation to shares and have a higher allocation to bonds. Those with a higher risk tolerance will have more shares in their portfolios and a greater allocation to emerging markets and alternatives.

In Chapter 19, I suggest some simple allocations that you might try, but believe me when I say that there is no single **correct** grouping of investment assets in a portfolio.

The most important factor?

Finally, there have been studies from Nobel Prize-winning economists which show asset allocation to be the single most important factor in determining the results from any portfolio of investments. The conclusions of the different studies vary widely, but on one point they all agree.

Being **in the market** is the key to investing success. No one gets rich by sitting on the sidelines wondering when or how to invest. Far better simply to start and get going. Yes, you might get the timing a bit wrong and buy into the market just before a downturn. But if you're investing for 20 years, who cares about the first six months? You have plenty of time to make more money in future.

I want you to understand the merits of asset allocation as you take your first steps as an investor, but more importantly I want you to understand that it is the markets that will help you build wealth over time. If you have a different asset allocation to me, our investments will behave differently, and that's OK. The only thing that matters is that you are moving towards your goals.

Everything you need to DO

1. Decide your level of interest

Other than to keep reading, I have only one thing that I suggest you do at this point, and that is to decide how much time you want to spend learning about and managing your investments.

Most people don't want to spend too much time – they would rather be hanging out with their kids, reading books, playing golf, whatever. For others, investing becomes a hobby and they take an avid interest every day in the goings-on of the stock market.

I have one client who has over 150 funds in his portfolio and whenever he comes in he presents me with a beautifully formatted spreadsheet showing the performance of each one. Other clients don't even look at their portfolio from one annual meeting with me to the next.

But what about you? Do you think you will want to spend much time on this, once you have set things up? In Chapter 19, I present some suggestions for both the hands-off person and the person who wants to get his or her hands a bit dirty.

The next three chapters, you'll be pleased to know, are shorter than the last two, and deal quickly with the next three levels of the investing process: funds, wrappers and platforms.

Chapter 15
Funds

B Y NOW YOU MAY BE thinking that you would like to invest in shares and bonds, and maybe one day into property. But if you do, you'll quickly come up against a problem – how do you actually buy a share? Is there a shop where you can walk in and walk out with some Vodafone shares, or a bar of gold?

It is possible to buy individual shares and bonds from a stockbroker, or even directly from the companies issuing them. You can even buy gold bars from the Royal Mint or a gold bullion company – just be sure to get a safe installed and upgrade your house contents insurance.

But many investors these days, rather than owning shares and bonds directly, hold them inside a fund.

Everything you need to KNOW

1. How a fund works

Let's say you live in a city and most of the time, public transport is perfectly adequate for your needs. You find that you occasionally feel the need for the use of a car, but not enough to justify the year-round costs of actually owning one. On talking to some of your friends, they feel the same way, and so you each put in some money and decide to buy a car between you. You will share the cost of insuring and servicing the car, and each pay for your own petrol use. In doing so, you have **pooled** your resources to buy a car from which you will all benefit. And you have probably bought a nicer car than you may have been able to on your own, because your friends' money has contributed to the cost.

A fund offers similar benefits to investors who want to buy shares, bonds or other assets. If you invest on your own, you will probably buy a handful of different shares before it becomes too much work to keep on top of your portfolio. But if you get your friends involved, you have a bigger pot of money to invest with, and you can therefore buy more shares than you could on your own.

Scale this up so that now there are hundreds of thousands of joint-owners in this fund. Imagine the size of the fund! How many shares could you buy with a fund of a billion pounds?!

Instead of owning the shares directly, you own units or shares in the fund, and the fund itself owns the shares. The price of your share in the fund is determined by the price of the underlying investments. Usually, fund share prices are set once a day.

Pooling your resources with other investors in this way affords you the following benefits.

Economies of scale

When buying and selling shares yourself, you will often pay dealing costs to a stockbroker or to the online system you use to deal. A fund with tens or hundreds of millions of pounds to invest can negotiate much lower fees from its brokers, or even afford to build its own trading systems to avoid paying fees to brokers at all.

The flip-side to this is that a fund has to be managed, and this comes at a cost. Fund management fees go to paying the fund manager and her team, the sales team, heating and lighting the offices, and creating brochures or flashy websites to attract prospective investors. Some funds are expensive and some are very low-cost.

Are there really economies of scale, once the net effect of the savings and costs is considered? The answer to this is yes, because funds allow you to buy far more shares than you ever could personally. This reduces the risk by spreading the money further than you could on your own.

Reduced paperwork

People who hold individual shares soon come to understand that they come with a great deal of paperwork, even in this digital age. You'll get prospectuses from the company which can run to hundreds of pages. You'll be sent the annual report on the company's performance and voting forms to reappoint the board and company accountants. If you own more than half a dozen shares this paperwork can become an avalanche coming through your letterbox.

If instead you hold a fund, all the share-owning paperwork is handled for you by the fund manager.

Reduced tax

If you hold shares directly, every time you buy and sell a shareholding you are potentially liable for capital gains tax. This potential tax liability is likely to affect your decision-making, adding another factor into your investment planning.

If you hold a fund on the other hand, and the fund manager decides to buy and sell some shares, there is no tax liability for you personally. You only incur tax if you sell out of the fund for a profit.

This doesn't apply if you hold your shares or funds within a pension or an ISA, as we shall see in the next chapter.

2. Types of funds

The most common type of fund in the UK is an **open-ended investment company**, called an **OEIC** (pronounced 'oik') for short.

The open-ended part of the name means that if more people want to invest, the fund can create more shares in the fund for those people. When someone wants to sell their investment, their shares in the fund are destroyed, so the number of shares in the fund is constantly changing.

This makes the structure very liquid. You can usually sell out of a fund on any working day, and receive the proceeds a few days later.

Unit trusts work similarly to OEICs but have one key difference in the form of something called a bid-offer spread. This means there is a difference between the price at which you buy units (the offer price) and the price at which you sell them (the bid price). Think of this as an initial charge for buying the units in the fund. In these days of increasing transparency and price pressures, most investors do well to avoid unit trusts.

Investment trusts are different again. They are closed-ended companies whose shares are traded on the stock market. This means that there is a finite number of shares in existence, which means that if you want to buy shares in an investment trust, you have to find someone willing to sell. When you want to sell, you have to find a buyer. This reduces the liquidity of investment trusts compared with their open-ended cousins, OEICs.

There are a couple of other differences with investment trusts. Firstly, an investment trust can borrow money to invest. This is called **gearing** and by definition it increases the risk of the fund because the borrowed money will have to be paid back. If the underlying investment bought with the borrowed money does not perform as hoped, then the fund could be in trouble.

Finally, the share price of an investment trust is affected by market sentiment rather than just the value of its underlying investments. Let's say that there are one million shares of the fund in existence and the value of all the underlying investments the fund has bought is £10 million. Each share would therefore be worth £10. But if the market doesn't like the outlook for the investment trust it might price the shares at only £9.50 each. This is called trading at a **discount**. If the market is positive about the fund and its shares are valued at £11 a share, this is called trading at a **premium.**

Finally, **exchange traded funds** or **ETFs** are very low-cost funds usually used to track a particular share market. They are a kind of hybrid between an investment trust and an ordinary share. ETFs are still funds which hold underlying investments, but rather than the fund holding assets chosen by a fund manager, they aim to track a given asset price, like gold, or an index, like the FTSE 100.

You need to take care with ETFs. They fall into two main types. **Physical** ETFs actually hold the underlying shares, just like an OEIC or investment trust. A **synthetic** ETF on the other hand will aim to track its market using complex financially engineered products you need PhD in economics to understand. As a rule, ordinary investors should avoid synthetic ETFs.

3. Passive versus active investing

This is a subject which elicits strong opinions amongst financial professionals. If you ever find yourself sitting next to a financial adviser at a wedding reception, don't ask them for their view on passive versus active investing – you'll never get away!

The difference is simple enough. Let's say you have decided that it is a really great idea to invest right now into companies in the FTSE 100 index. These are the 100 largest companies registered in the UK, and include well-known companies such as Vodafone, Barclays and BP.

An **active** investor would take a look at those 100 companies and decide which specific ones to buy, hold and sell at any one time, with the intention of producing a superior investment performance by being actively selective. This superior investment performance is usually defined by trying to beat a stated market index, or benchmark (such as the FTSE 100).

A **passive** investor would just buy shares in all 100 companies. The intention here is to achieve the performance of the FTSE 100 index companies as a whole.

Active investing requires research and insight into the workings of the companies you are investing into. It also requires skill, experience and luck. An actively managed fund will have a very well-paid fund manager backed by a team of analysts. The costs of these have to be covered by the investors into the fund.

Passive investing simply requires the fund manager to match the fund's investments with the market as a whole each day. This can be done largely by computer algorithm, removing a lot of cost from the process, and making this form of investing cheaper for investors. Passive funds are often known as index funds, tracker funds, or just trackers.

Active investors try to beat the market. Passive investors aim to track or match the market.

Which is best?

They both have merit. Investing in actively managed funds introduces an extra level of risk to your investing – the risk that you might choose the wrong manager. Academic studies have suggested that only one-in-four managers consistently performs better than their benchmark over three years. Over longer periods, only one in 100 managers outperforms. That means there is a very good chance you'll choose a manager who is underperforming at any given time.

Choosing to invest passively removes the risk of choosing the wrong manager. If we believe that it is markets that make you money over time, why not just track the markets rather than try to beat them?

I strongly believe that most ordinary investors are best served by opting for a passive investment strategy. It keeps your costs down and reduces the amount of research you need to do.

Everything you need to DO

1. Re-read this chapter

If your mind is blown right now with all this information, don't worry. You can always go back over things again and take your time to digest it.

But I want you to understand all these terms so that you invest from a position of knowledge. Doing that gives you the best chance to make good decisions that will serve you well.

Other than that, there are no practical steps to take at this point, so let's move on.

Chapter 16
Wrappers

LET'S RECAP. YOU INVEST INTO **assets** by buying **funds** to get the benefits of economies of scale, increased liquidity and so on.

Wrappers are the next level up. Think of these as boxes into which you put your investments to gain various benefits. The key things that distinguish one wrapper from another are tax treatment and access.

Everything you need to KNOW

1. The main wrapper types

As with much of personal finance, there are way more wrapper types than most people will ever use, but you need to know the main ones you're likely to come across. These are as follows:

⇨ **General investment account (GIA)** – these are the basic form of account. They have no special tax advantages or access limitations. You will use these only if you exceed the amounts you can put into other wrappers.

⇨ **Individual savings account (ISA)** – these accounts are entirely free of both income and capital gains taxes (don't worry, we're going to cover these taxes in Chapter 18). ISAs are super useful and will form the backbone of your wealth-building process.

⇨ **Pension** – if there's one subject in personal finance that breeds both confusion and strong emotions, it's pensions. At their simplest (and we'll go deeper in a minute), a pension is a place to save money until you retire. You get tax breaks from the government for investing into a pension, but you pay tax when you take money out eventually. Pensions can be personal or occupational – that is, provided by your employer.

⇨ **Investment bond** – these are technically contracts of life insurance, but they're investments really. They have fallen out of favour in recent years, but they still have some benefits particularly when used within trusts. They also have some tax advantages for higher-rate taxpayers.

⇨ **Venture capital trust (VCT)** – these are wrappers in which you hold investments in small companies. In return for you helping to boost the backbone of the UK economy, the government gives very beneficial tax-breaks. The downside is that VCT investments are risky and the money is locked in for five years.

⇨ **Enterprise investment schemes (EIS)** – these are similar to VCTs, but with slightly different limits and tax breaks. The minimum term is three years. They are also designed to be invested into specific assets which can be less liquid and more volatile than ordinary shares.

Of all of these, most people will only need to use a pension and an ISA, so I want to focus on these two alone. Remember, this book isn't meant to be exhaustive. If you think your situation may require you to invest in the other wrapper types, I urge you to seek professional financial advice. I show you how to go about finding an adviser towards the end of this book.

2. All about ISAs

ISAs are the simplest, most accessible, easiest to understand wrapper. When thinking about wrappers, you need to understand the tax situation at three different points:

1. **In** – when you contribute, or put money in.

2. **During** – while the money is in the wrapper.

3. **Out** – when you withdraw, or take money out.

ISAs are straightforward enough:

⇨ **In** – there are no special tax breaks for putting money into an ISA, with the sole exception of the Lifetime ISA, of which more in a minute. The money you put in has likely already been taxed when you earned it. There is an annual contribution limit into ISAs, which at the time of writing in 2018 is £20,000. You don't have to invest the full amount; you can put anything up to that full amount into an ISA in any one tax year.

⇨ **During** – while money in an ISA grows, it does so entirely free of income tax and capital gains tax – a useful benefit.

⇨ **Out** – whenever you withdraw money from an ISA, there is no tax to pay whatsoever.

As you can see, there are some key benefits here. £20,000 per year can be salted away and most ordinary folks won't save more than that in any one year. That's why the ISA is the most commonly used savings and investment account in the UK.

While ISAs are simple enough in principle, there are currently **five** main types:

1. **Cash ISA** – a tax-free bank account, which could be an excellent place to keep your emergency fund.

2. **Stocks & shares ISA** – here you can invest into shares, bonds, and quite a few other asset classes.

3. **Innovative finance ISA** – a sub-brand of the ISA family introduced in 2016 to allow investment into peer-to-peer lending investments, a niche but growing investment approach.

4. **Junior ISA** – a tax-free savings account for children which can hold both cash and stocks and shares. The money belongs to the child once they reach age 16, but they can't withdraw it until they are 18. The maximum that can be put into a Junior ISA in the 2018/19 tax year is £4260.

5. **Lifetime ISA** – a special ISA with an extra perk. If you're aged between 18 and 40, you can invest up to £4000, to which the government will add a 25% bonus, up to a maximum of £1000 per year. Yep, that's free money from the government, but it comes with a caveat. You can withdraw money for buying your first house or after age 60 without any penalties. If you withdraw for any other reason, you will have to pay back the government bonus. The £4000 annual Lifetime ISA allowance takes up part of your overall ISA allowance, leaving you £16,000 to invest in other ISAs. A similar scheme called a **Help to Buy ISA** will close in 2019, and is less attractive than the Lifetime ISA.

3. All about pensions

As I said before, pensions are often misunderstood, but they needn't be. You just need to get your head around a couple of basic principles.

Money purchase and final salary pensions

A money purchase pension (more properly called a **defined contribution** pension) is the kind of scheme where you build up a pot of money over your working life. With these schemes, you know what you will put in to the pension but you don't know what you will get out of it.

Money purchase pensions are essentially saving and investment plans, so most people use them to hold investment funds, just like an ISA.

The alternative is the final salary scheme, more properly called a **defined benefit** pension. Here, it doesn't really matter what gets put in, because the scheme provides a defined benefit – a promise of a future income. You know what you'll get from day one in your retirement and, as such, these are extremely valuable and increasingly rare schemes. These days, they are mostly the preserve of public sector employers, like the NHS or police service.

Personal and occupational pensions

As the name occupational pension suggests, many employers provide pension schemes into which you can contribute. These schemes can be either defined contribution or defined benefit.

Personal schemes are pension plans that you set up yourself and they are always defined contribution schemes.

I should pause here to mention that the world of pensions is perhaps the most complex area of personal financial planning. While pensions these days are fairly straightforward for most of us, if you have a pension plan from any earlier than the mid-1990s, there may be all kinds of weird bells and whistles attached, some good some bad.

That means that most people under 40 reading this will probably not have more complex and esoteric schemes. If you think you might have a pension like this, you should definitely seek professional advice to get the best out of it. I have a podcast episode on this very subject at meaningfulmoney.tv/BQ9.

Self-invested personal pension

There's another kind of personal pension called a self-invested personal pension (or SIPP). This has the capability to hold more complex investments like commercial property, which are excluded under other types of pension. A SIPP can be more expensive than an ordinary pension, but only if you use the extra capability.

Auto-enrolment

It is now the law that employers have to provide and pay into a pension scheme for their employees and automatically enrol their staff into the scheme. (An exception is that some lower-paid staff don't have to be enrolled in the scheme.) The employee can opt-out of the pension, but they will be automatically enrolled again after three years. This is the government's attempt to get more of us saving for our retirement and early indications show that it is working.

Tax treatment of pensions

Here is the tax treatment of pensions:

⇨ **In** – money paid into a pension will benefit from tax-relief. That means that the government will add to your contribution. When you pay into a pension, the pension company you invest with will request the top-up from HMRC. If you are a higher rate taxpayer, you will get additional tax back through your tax return.

⇨ **During** – while money in a pension grows, it does so entirely free of income tax and capital gains tax.

⇨ **Out** – whenever you withdraw money from a pension plan, it is taxed as if it was earnings from a job. There may be also be a tax-free cash lump sum payable. You cannot withdraw money from a personal pension until at least age 55. For many occupational pension schemes this date is later, more usually 60 or 65.

Annual allowance and lifetime allowance

Because there is a real benefit in paying into pensions thanks to the government tax relief, there is a limit on how much you can put into a pension in any one year, called the annual allowance. You are also limited by the amount you earn.

The maximum you can pay into a pension is the annual allowance or 100% of your 'net relevant earnings', whichever is lower. If you haven't fully used your annual allowance in the previous three years, you can

carry forward that unused allowance, but the total amount you can pay in is still limited to your earnings in that year, even if you are using carry forward.

If you are in a final salary pension, it works differently. You will receive a statement each year showing how your increased benefit in that year matches up to the annual allowance. If you contribute more than the annual allowance, you will have to pay a tax charge.

The government also places a limit on the amount you can hold in pensions over a lifetime, called the lifetime allowance. This means you can't have more than this in your combined pension funds without paying a tax charge.

The size of your pension fund is only tested against the lifetime allowance when you come to take benefits in retirement, or if you die before age 75. The lifetime allowance has changed over recent years, which is why I haven't quoted a figure here. Whenever it has changed, HMRC have allowed pension holders to lock in the higher lifetime allowance, but this comes with some compromises, such as no longer being able to add to your pension.

I imagine that most people in this position won't be reading a book about the basics of personal finance, so let's move on!

For most of us who are not yet retired, that's all you really need to know about pensions. There is so much more to tell, but it really isn't necessary for most of us to dig any deeper than that.

Everything you need to DO

1. Join your workplace pension (occupational pension)

This is about as close anything in personal finance gets to being a no-brainer. If your employer provides a pension scheme (and under the auto-enrolment rules they almost certainly will) **you should join it**.

At Jacksons Wealth, we have some companies as clients and we manage their pension schemes. When we go in and speak to new employees about joining the scheme, there is understandably some reluctance. Many people, particularly young adults earning a proper wage for the first time, are reluctant to give even a small part of this up. But when we tell them that their employer will often match their contribution, and that the government will also pay in for them in the form of tax relief, they often change their tune.

And that really is the crux of it – why would you turn down free money? Yes, the free money can't be accessed until you are aged 55 at least, but that's great! Think of how much the money is going to grow over that time. Believe me, when dealing with clients who are retiring, I have never had anyone say to me that they wish they had put less money into their pension. They always wish they had contributed more!

Now, if you work for yourself, there obviously isn't a generous boss putting money into your pension for you. But you can still open a pension and begin getting the tax relief from the government. You should do that as soon as possible. It doesn't need to be a complicated plan with lots of options. A simple personal pension, sometimes called a stakeholder pension, will do just fine. Many insurance companies offer these and there are lots of online pension providers these days too. It's more important to start saving than it is to worry too much about the specific pension you choose.

How much should you put in? Hold that thought for one minute, while I address the next thing you need to do.

2. Decide on your total savings rate

I firmly believe that you shouldn't worry too much about saving and investing until you are clear of bad debt and have some kind of emergency fund in place. If you try to do everything at once, you're in danger of spreading yourself too thin. I know you want to get started with your investing, but be patient. When you are ready, you can go all-in and really take it seriously, knowing that you're building wealth for yourself, not someone else.

In the spirit of paying yourself first, you should decide how much you are going to save – as we saw in Step One – and put that much into your investments (whether that is a pension or ISA) as soon as you can at the start of the month.

Remember our rule of thumb from back in Chapter 4? Try and aim for your age minus 15 as a savings rate. So if you are aged 40, aim to save 25% of your income after tax.

If you are in a workplace pension, you should be able to see how much you are paying into that scheme by looking at your payslip. Don't include your employer's contribution, just your own. Take this off your savings rate to determine how much you should be saving from your net income.

Here's an example. A 40-year-old wants to save 25% of her £2,000 per month net income – that's £500 per month. She is paying £150 per month into her workplace pension, which means she needs to save £350 per month to reach her savings rate goal.

In this case, she could ask her employer about increasing the amount she pays into her pension, and how much, if any, the employer will match. Any savings after that should be directed into an ISA once per month after she has been paid her salary.

3. Decide on the split between pensions and ISAs

Should you add more money into your pension or start with an ISA? As ever, the answer to that depends quite a bit on your life stage.

If you are young with no dependents, or in a couple with no kids, I would err very much on the side of paying into ISAs rather than pensions. Sure, join your employer's pension, but after that, stick with an ISA for the first few years.

If there isn't an employer's scheme available to you, you should still take out a pension, but I would pay maybe a quarter of your total savings budget into that, with the rest into an ISA.

The thinking here is that there is still lots of opportunity for life to change, and locking money up until age 55 makes less sense than keeping it available.

Yes, you will make more money in pensions because of the tax relief when you put money in. That extra money from the government, and possibly from your employer too, grows over time, whereas with an ISA, you're on your own – no one will put money in for you, with the exception of the Lifetime ISA.

As you get older and your ISA portfolio begins to grow nicely, you can begin to shift the balance more towards pensions. For me, who has been married for 20 years, and whose kids are now in their late teens, I am investing more into pensions than ISAs. I have enough available money in ISAs and so I am happy to lock up more of my regular savings into pensions.

Know yourself though. If you think that you may be tempted to dip into ISAs too much, then weight your savings towards pensions, where you can't get at the money until age 55 at the earliest.

Every single person and family reading this will be different. For example, if you want to send your kids to private secondary school, you're likely to put as much as you can into investments in an accessible wrapper like an ISA until your kids have left school, and only then will you focus on pensions. You would prioritise saving into ISAs, while paying the minimum into your pension to get the employer's match and the tax relief. Then later, you would start to make more savings into pensions.

Chapter 17
Platforms

T HE TOP-MOST LEVEL IS THE platform. This is entirely optional for many people, but there are benefits to platform use which I'll cover shortly.

When I first started in personal finance 20 years ago, there really wasn't such a thing as a platform. Back then, there were so-called fund supermarkets, where you could access lots of different fund managers within one wrapper at a time, but nowadays things have got a bit more exciting.

Everything you need to KNOW

1. A platform is an administrative system for investments

Modern platforms are incredibly powerful systems. The best ones offer lots of different kinds of tax wrappers, from pensions and ISAs through to onshore and offshore investment bonds and even cash management tools like fixed-term deposit accounts.

They also provide access to hundreds or even thousands of different kinds of funds, invested all over the world. They offer research tools to help you choose your investments and also provide detailed transaction histories and tax-planning tools.

I really like the convenience of a platform. My platform of choice has a superb iPhone app that I can log into with my fingerprint so I can see the value of my holdings at any time and even place a trade to shift some money around if I want to.

2. Platform costs

Platforms really are one-stop shops for most investors and best of all, they are transparent when it comes to cost. Of course, some are more expensive than others, and some provide more functionality than others.

Most platforms charge a percentage of the money you hold with them, so as you invest more, you pay more. Others charge a fixed fee, which is obviously better for larger accounts.

You are paying primarily for convenience, particularly if you have a larger portfolio which takes a bit of managing. Doing so on a platform can save a lot of time and hassle. I have clients with ISA and pension accounts with as many as 15 different providers, and it is a pain to stay on top of it all. Most people prefer the convenience of the one-stop shop, even if it does come at a cost.

3. Platforms are entirely optional

That said, it may be that you don't bother with a platform. If you have a pension at work, that's pretty much taken care of. And so you're left with a choice of companies with whom to open an ISA. As this is likely to be the only account you hold for the foreseeable future, why go to the expense of paying for a system which is able to cope with complex portfolios, only to hold one simple account?

It does depend a little bit as to what you want to get up to with your underlying investments. If you want to take a really hands-on approach, researching and choosing funds and moving money around throughout your life, then you would enjoy the benefits of a platform. If instead you just want to put the money away, choose a fund or two and let the thing run, then you probably don't need to pay for a platform.

Everything you need to DO

1. Decide on your needs

The first step in choosing a platform is to decide what kind of facilities you might need.

If you are just getting started investing monthly into an ISA, then you may not need a platform at all. You could decide on a fund you like the look of and open your ISA directly with the fund provider, saving yourself the platform fees.

If you think you will enjoy exploring different investment opportunities, then you want a platform which enables easy switching of investments and doesn't charge transaction fees.

The size of your portfolio will also play a part in this decision. Most people with larger portfolios want to diversify by using a few different funds with different fund management companies. This can bring paperwork headaches, as you have to deal with several companies. A platform can remedy this by still offering access to lots of different fund managers, but consolidating the reporting, so you get one statement with all your investment funds listed.

2. Do some research

As with anything these days there are plenty of places to research the best home for your money. As you have decided what features you might want to make use of, you can look for those features and compare one platform with another.

Ask your friends and social networks for recommendations and follow up on the suggestions. Buy and read investing magazines and look for articles reviewing the different platforms. Start with a simple Google search for 'investment platform research' and follow the links from there.

The best place I know of for non-financial advisers to research the platform market is the website of financial industry consultancy **the lang cat**.[12] Go to their site and search for publications. Each year they produce an independent guide to the platform market called 'Come And Have A Go' – they're quirky like that. Best of all, it's free.

3. Open an account

All of the platform providers make it very easy to open accounts. They may have slightly different minimum lump sum and monthly investment amounts, which might influence your choice. But after that, it's just a case of logging on, opening an account and setting up a direct debit. You can send any lump sum savings across to your account directly from your bank account.

Don't leave this too long. It's easy to spend ages researching and planning to the nth degree, but remember inertia risk – that's the danger here. All platforms make it easy to get your money back out, or transfer to another provider, subject to the accessibility rules and possible transfer fees of the wrappers themselves, such as pensions. It doesn't have to be a one-off decision which you are stuck with forever.

4. Consider consolidation

If you have a bunch of ISAs already, or a couple of neglected pension plans, now is a good time to consider consolidating these onto a platform.

---

[12] www.langcatfinancial.co.uk

It is always worth comparing the costs of doing so. If you have pensions that are pretty old, there may be benefits that you will lose if you transfer them to another provider like a platform. Always call your existing pension provider and ask them 'are there any important benefits that I will lose if I transfer this plan away?'

In my experience with clients, plans which are neglected and forgotten about can be a real drag on your wealth-building goals. Far better to have a clear plan – be intentional! – and bring things together where you can watch them grow and stay engaged.

Chapter 18
A Word About Tax

BEFORE I ROUND THINGS OFF by giving you the practical steps that will serve 95% of all people looking to build wealth over the long term, we need to talk about tax.

Tax is unavoidable. And in fact, we wouldn't want to avoid it. Tax is the mechanism by which developed governments collect money from the population to pay for the services which we all use. Roads, hospitals, state pensions, prisons and the government itself are all sustained by the collection and distribution of tax. My view is that if you enjoy the society that tax provides, then you should pay your fair share.

We have talked a little bit about the tax breaks provided by ISAs and pensions. This is entirely legitimate tax planning. The government knows that if they incentivise saving into such schemes with tax benefits, the nation will be financially healthier as a result.

This brief chapter is intended as an introduction to the three main taxes.

Everything you need to KNOW

1. Income tax and National Insurance

Income tax is payable on money earned from various sources:

⇨ Salary

⇨ Pensions

⇨ Commission, bonuses or other benefits from work

⇨ Rent from property

⇨ Interest on money saved in bank or building society accounts

⇨ Dividends from shares or funds (held outside pensions and ISAs)

Everyone has a personal allowance, which is an amount that you can earn each year without paying any tax at all.

Income in excess of the personal allowance is taxed at different rates, depending on how much you earn. The three different rates are called basic, higher and additional rate tax, and as I write this in early 2018, they are taxed at 20%, 40% and 45% respectively. High earners with income over £100,000 will also see their personal allowance gradually removed the more they earn.

To complicate things a little, dividends are taxed at different rates to the other sources of income, and both dividends and interest have their own special personal allowances on top of the one that everyone gets.

Imagine a wall with markings in chalk showing the personal allowance and the basic, higher and additional income tax rates.

Now imagine we stack some boxes against the wall, one on top of the other. The first box will be your earnings from your work, or if you're over a certain age, your pensions. If the height of that box is higher than the personal allowance chalk line, you will pay some tax.

Add another box on top of that to represent the rent you receive from an investment property, another on top of that for some interest and yet another to represent some dividends on shares held outside an ISA.

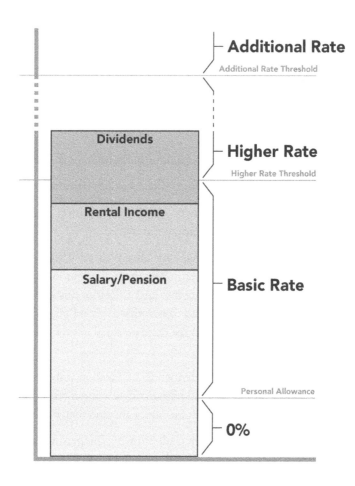

As the boxes stack up, one on top of the other, we can see that they come up to various points in our chalk scale on the wall. If your salary takes you nearly into the higher rate tax band, dividends might just tip you into it, and will be part taxed at the basic rate and partly at the higher rate. The order of stacking the boxes is important and coincides with the order of the bullet points when I listed the income sources above.

Finally, National Insurance is not insurance at all. It's a form of income tax payable on your earnings from your occupation.

2. Capital gains tax

Capital gains tax is quite a bit more straightforward than income tax, you'll be pleased to know.

If you sell an asset for a profit, then you are potentially liable for capital gains tax. Again, everyone gets an annual allowance that they can gain tax free every tax year (6 April to 5 April). If you make a gain which is more than the annual allowance, then the amount of the excess gain is added to your income and taxed accordingly. Confusingly, the tax rates are different than for income tax and different again when you make a gain on selling a rental property, rather than, say, selling shares. Capital gains tax is never chargeable when you sell your main home.

That's about it. Sell something for a profit, take off the annual allowance, pay tax on the rest – simple.

3. Inheritance tax

Inheritance tax is only payable when you die, and only if the value of the stuff you own is worth more than the so-called Nil Rate Band. Whatever the value of your estate in excess of the Nil Rate Band is taxed at 40% **unless**:

⇨ You leave it to your spouse or civil partner.

⇨ You leave it to charity.

Also, if you have a house and you plan to leave it to your direct descendants after you die, then there is an extra tax-free amount called the Residence Nil Rate Band.

4. Is that it?

In a word, no. There is loads more information that I could go into when it comes to taxation, but the detail above is what you need to know at this point, when you're getting started with financial planning. You can always get more detail from the gov.uk website or from MeaningfulMoney, where I have videos and podcasts explaining things in more detail.

You'll notice that I have shied away from figures such as the amount of the income tax personal allowance or the tax rates on capital gains tax. That's because these figures change from year to year, it seems. There are also differences in Scotland compared to England, Wales and Northern Ireland. To include all the differences would be difficult to read and also out of date the minute this book is printed.

The rates I have included are ones which seem to have stuck for many years without being tweaked. But they may change in future – that's the nature of the beast.

Everything you need to DO

1. Use pensions and ISAs

The main reason that most people should use pensions and ISAs is because of the tax breaks that are available to everyone using these wrappers.

The vast majority of people reading this book will never be in a position to save the full ISA allowance *and* the full pension allowance in one year. And so they will never need to look any further than these very tax-efficient vehicles.

Saving into an ISA and pension is the best way to avoid income and capital gains taxes, and chances are, if you're just getting going with building your financial future, you don't need to worry too much about inheritance tax at this point.

OK. We have covered asset classes, funds, wrappers and platforms, and the basics of taxation. Knowing this, we now need to bring it all together into the final and most important **Everything you need to DO** section.

The suggestions I make in the next chapter will be sufficient for almost everyone reading this book. I make suggestions for those who want to be hands-off with their wealth-building and also for those who want to take an active interest.

Let's do this!

Chapter 19
Practical Investing

L ET'S ROUND OFF THE LAST of our three steps by giving you some clear actions to take to start investing.

It may be that you can apply some of this stuff in your ISA, but not in your work pension, which may not give you as much flexibility. Take what you learn in this chapter and apply it **as well as you can** within the limits of the tools available to you.

Remember to pay yourself first by setting up payments to go out from your bank account and into your investment account (most likely an ISA) as soon as you get paid.

After that, I have two courses of action for two kinds of people, those who are relaxed and hands-off, and those who want to take an active part in building and maintaining their investments.

We'll look at these in turn.

For the hands-off folks

You guys are so chilled. You are the ones who want to set things up right and are happy to review them once a year, but for the rest of the time, you're happy to let your finances look after themselves.

For what it is worth, I fall squarely into this category of people. I spend my days managing other people's financial affairs, so I don't want to spend my precious personal time agonising over which fund to buy and whether the emerging markets will outperform the developed world next year. I check the values of my pension and ISA once each month, just to keep my records up to date, and I review things a bit more formally once a year. I'll cover what that review involves later in this chapter.

1. Choose a multi-asset portfolio fund

Remember back to all the stuff we covered about asset allocation, fund choice, and regular reviews – sounds like a lot of work, right? But what if all that could be done for you?

The good news is that a **multi-asset portfolio fund** will spread your money across different kinds of assets, and across the whole world all in one convenient off-the-shelf package.

These kinds of funds have really taken off in recent years, and they are available from a range of different fund managers.

Here's what to look for.

Firstly, you can find these funds in four investment **sectors**. The Investment Association has divided the entire universe of funds available in the UK into sectors. All the funds in a given sector will have a similar approach, and the idea is that by grouping them together, you can easily compare similar funds against each other. The four sectors you are looking for when researching a multi-asset portfolio fund are:

1. Mixed Investment 0–35% Shares

2. Mixed Investment 20–60% Shares

3. Mixed Investment 40–85% Shares

4. Flexible Investment

The first thing you may notice here is that there is some overlap between those sectors. A fund with 50% of its money in shares could fall into either the 20–60% sector or the 40–85% sector. This is because the sectors are about applying limits to how much equity exposure a fund can have if it wants to stay in that sector.

Most funds adjust the level of equity exposure depending on their view about the economy at any given time. If they are concerned about share prices falling, they may reduce their exposure to equities. But a fund in the 20-60% equities sector could never reduce its exposure to shares below 20% or else it would have to move to a different sector, which would require the fund manager to notify all shareholders of that fund.

The funds you're after will often have names that refer either to the split of assets, or to the kind of risk profile they are suitable for. You may see names like the Vanguard LifeStrategy 60% Equity fund, or the 7IM Balanced fund. Sometimes the names are not so obviously linked to the makeup of the fund, like the Legal & General Multi-Index 3 fund.

If you have established your general attitude to risk, you should be able to find a fund which matches:

⇨ If you are a more **cautious** investor, look for a fund in the **Mixed Investment 0–35% Shares** sector.

⇨ If you are a **balanced** or moderate risk investor, look for a fund in the **Mixed Investment 20–60% Shares** sector

⇨ If you are a more **adventurous** investor, look for a fund in the **Mixed Investment 40–85% Shares** sector or the **Flexible Investment** sector.

Once you have identified one or more suitable candidate funds, read all you can about them.

How widely does each fund spread your money around? Generally, a wider spread of investments means lower risk.

How long has it been around and how large is the fund compared with its peers? Often, a larger fund with a longer track record is a better bet than a newer fund without the proven history.

Compare the costs of your contenders. Look for a figure called the OCF, or ongoing charges figure. Passively managed funds are likely to be below 0.75% per year, with actively managed funds costing anything up to 1.5% per year. When starting out, I would opt for passively managed funds.

And of course, you can start to look at how each fund has performed. Every piece of literature produced by the investment industry will contain the same sentence somewhere at the bottom. It goes like this:

"Past performance is no guide to future performance"

Of course, that's absolutely true. Just because a fund made 10% last year doesn't mean it'll do that in the future. There are a million variables which will affect performance, from manager decisions to market movements. However, the way the fund has performed in the past relative to what was going on in the wider world **can** be something of a guide to how it **might** behave in future.

For example, if markets have been on a recent surge of strong performance, and your prospective fund choice has not performed well in that time, then you should ask why. Was the manager caught off guard? Was the asset allocation 'off' in some way so that the manager didn't catch the rise? It's always worth asking the important question 'Why?' when considering a fund's performance.

Look at how each fund has performed over longer time periods. It doesn't matter at all how well the fund has done over the past month. You're going to be investing for decades, most likely, so a month's performance is irrelevant. Instead, look at three-, five- and even ten-year performance and look for consistency of returns.

Remember, you're not investing money you're going to need in the next three or four years – that money goes into the bank. Investing is a long-term game and so when choosing funds you should look at performance over long time periods.

It can be useful to compare your prospective choice of funds with other funds in the same peer group. The factsheets that all funds are obliged to provide will often show you the **quartile ranking** of the fund over different timescales. This divides the funds in a sector into the top 25% of performers, the second 25%, the third and the fourth. So a first quartile fund over three years has performed better than 75% of its peers over the time period.

Look for funds which are consistently second quartile and above. In my experience these funds are often better at controlling the volatility of their performance over time. They're comfortably above average, but not looking to shoot the lights out. That's a good place to be for a predictable investment return over time.

You can find quartile rankings using research tools on your chosen platform, or you can use websites like FE Trustnet and Morningstar, both of which are free, but also have paid versions with more capable tools.

For the hands-off folks, that's about all you need to do. Whether you are saving into a pension or ISA or both, find a multi-asset portfolio fund, or maybe two, and begin investing into that fund regularly. As your money grows you may decide to add in a second fund or a third, to provide some diversification, but it doesn't need to get any more complex than that. You can now skip ahead to the section 'For everyone', below.

For the more hands-on folks

The multi-asset funds we have just looked at are a great way to hand over the heavy lifting of investing to someone else. You just have to choose a fund and keep an eye on things as you go on.

But maybe you are someone who fancies delving a little deeper into the mechanics of creating and maintaining a portfolio? What should you do differently?

1. Identify your asset allocation

I'm assuming that you have identified your personal risk tolerance. Once that's done, you need to put together an asset allocation which matches. Below I have provided some examples which could act as a starting point for you.

Cautious

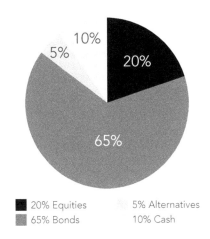

■ 20% Equities   5% Alternatives
■ 65% Bonds   10% Cash

Moderately cautious

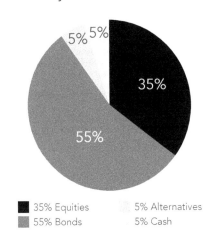

■ 35% Equities   5% Alternatives
■ 55% Bonds   5% Cash

Balanced

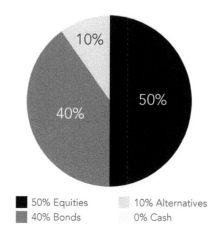

■ 50% Equities   ░ 10% Alternatives
■ 40% Bonds   □ 0% Cash

Moderately adventurous

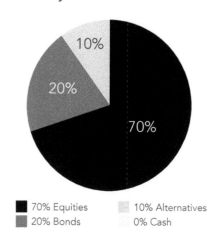

■ 70% Equities   ░ 10% Alternatives
■ 20% Bonds   □ 0% Cash

Adventurous

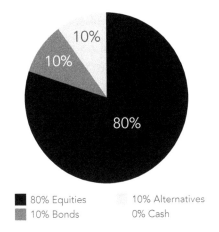

80% Equities 10% Alternatives
10% Bonds 0% Cash

Remember that there is no single correct asset allocation, but I have backtested the allocations above and they have performed as expected in the past. What the future holds, I don't know. Just remember, you are responsible for any decisions you make in this regard and the diagrams here are for illustrative purposes only.

2. Choose tracker funds or ETFs to fill up your asset allocation

Once you have identified how much of your portfolio you should allocate to each different asset, you need to choose a fund or two to fill up that portion of your allocation.

I suggest you do this using tracker funds at first, because they are the most straightforward method of investing passively, then perhaps moving on to include more technically complex exchange traded funds (ETFs) later, as you become more experienced.

To find a tracker fund in the right category, you need to look at the Investment Association sectors. I've included a diagram showing all the IA sectors overleaf. You can see that there are two main groups called Income and Growth, and within those there are some sub-groups.

If you are a investor looking to build wealth over the long term, and you were looking to fill up your UK allocation, you could look in the UK All Companies or UK Smaller Companies sectors.

Use research tools on your platform of choice, or on FE Trustnet or Morningstar, to filter down the choices using these sectors first of all. Then use a costs filter to remove all funds charging more than 0.5% per year OCF. This will whittle down the field so that only tracker funds remain, with a few exceptions maybe.

Make sure each fund you look at is indeed a tracker, rather than an active fund. Look for words like *tracker* or *index* in the fund name and always check the description.

Identify a few possible candidates and look at each one carefully, comparing things like performance, charges, and fund size.

You should also consider the **tracking error**, which is a measure of how closely the fund tracks its target market. The smaller the number, the closer the tracking, and the more effective the fund.

Don't spend too much time or lose sleep over this. There won't be a great deal to choose between most tracker funds, so if you find yourself going round in circles, just pick one. You can always review how it does versus its peers as you go along. For now, just get going, and remember that being in the market is the most important thing.

Repeat this process for every slice of your asset allocation pie until you have a handful of tracker funds you can invest into. For the larger slices of, say, more than 20% of the portfolio, you might want to consider using a couple of funds; for the smaller slices, one fund will do.

Guide to Investment Sectors

All Sectors

These four groups determine what the underlying funds are intending to achieve

| Capital Protection | Income | Growth | Specialist |

These sub-groups indicate the primary asset class the underlying fund invests in

| | Fixed Income | Equity | Mixed Asset | Equity | Mixed Asset | |

Capital Protection	Fixed Income	Equity	Mixed Asset	Equity	Mixed Asset	Specialist
Money Market	UK Gilts	UK Equity Income	UK Equity & Bond Income	UK All Companies	Mixed Investment 0-35% Shares	Personal Pensions
Short Term Money Market	UK Indexed Linked Gilts	Global Equity Income		UK Smaller Companies	Mixed Investment 20-60% Shares	Property
Protected	Sterling Corporate Bond			Japan	Mixed Investment 40-85% Shares	Specialist
	Sterling Strategic Bond			Japanese Smaller Companies	Flexible Investment	Targeted Absolute Return
	Sterling High Yield Bond			Asia Pacific Inc Japan		Technology & Telecommunications
	Global Bonds			Asia Pacific Exc Japan		
	Global Emerging Market Bonds			China/Greater China		
				North America		
				North American Smaller Cos		
				Europe Excluding UK		
				Europe Including UK		
				European Smaller Cos		
				Global		
				Global Emerging Markets		

For everyone

1. Diversify using core and satellite investing

Whether you opt for a done-for-you portfolio fund, or build a portfolio of funds yourself, you can take things a step further by using a core and satellite approach.

This approach has the main bulk of your money invested in either portfolio funds, or a collection of trackers as I've described. But outside this core of the portfolio there is a smaller proportion, the satellite, invested differently.

This can work in a couple of distinct ways. You can opt for a passive multi-asset core to your portfolio and an actively managed satellite. Or your core could be your chosen set of tracker funds, and your satellite be made up of really focussed investments such as a gold fund. You could even stock your satellite portion with more esoteric investments like peer-to-peer lending perhaps.

Don't have your satellite as more than 15% of your total portfolio, and 10% is probably better. If your chosen satellite holdings do extremely well and end up representing 25% of your total portfolio, don't drink your own Kool-Aid, as the Americans say. Chances are you got lucky, and you are not the next Warren Buffett after all. Sell down some of your satellite and buy into your core to get the percentages back into balance.

2. Embrace the principle of risk-flexing

Remember back in Chapter 13 when we talked about timescale and risk? You can apply this to the different elements of your investing in a simple way.

Let's say you are a balanced investor aged 35 looking to build wealth for your retirement one day. You're looking at a timescale of at least 20 years, and more likely 25–30 years. Given that length of time over which your money will be invested, you could consider increasing the risk of your portfolio, if you feel able.

I call this risk-flexing, where you take your own risk tolerance as a starting point, and then flex it up or down depending on the timescales involved. Take a look at the table below.

	< 2 years	2-4 years	4-5 years	5-10 years	10+ years
Accumulation (Building Wealth)	Risk-free	Risk-free	Risk Profile - 1	Risk Profile	Risk Profile + 1

	< 2 years	2-4 years	4-8 years	8+ years	£ you'll never need
Decumulation (Spending)	Risk-free	Risk Profile -1	Risk Profile	Risk Profile + 1	Take Your Pick

As a balanced wealth-builder investing over 20 years, you could consider investing according to your Balanced risk profile **plus one step**, which I'll call Moderately Adventurous.

When you get to within ten years of your goal, you could flex the risk of your portfolio down a notch to Balanced. And then as you get within five years of your goal, you could flex down further, to Moderately Cautious, until eventually you're in a low-risk environment.

Some pension providers do this automatically for you, and they often call it *lifestyling*. As a rule I don't like that approach because it is **automatic**. I would rather consider timescales, asset allocations and risk profiles intentionally (that word again) each time I review my portfolio.

You'll notice I have put different timescales on the wealth-building and wealth-enjoying phases of life. This is because it is important not to take too little risk in retirement – you don't want to outlive your money.

There is an increasing body of research which indicates that it makes more sense to keep the risk of your investments higher in retirement than your intuition might suggest that you do. This is an area for a discussion with a competent financial planner, who can help you understand the implications of living too long or investing too cautiously. As I've mentioned before, this book does not cover in detail the considerations of those who are imminently approaching retirement; if this applies to you then you should look elsewhere for information.

3. Review regularly

I suggest that you formally review how things are going once a year. You can review things six-monthly if you like, but more regularly than that is not necessary.

What should you measure to determine if you're on track or not?

For the first three years I would track the performance of your portfolio as a whole, rather than worrying too much about the component parts. If you're new to this, you need to spend that time reading and learning as much as you can about what's going on in the world and watching how markets and your portfolio respond to those world events.

From year four onwards you should consider three main points.

Firstly, reassess your timescale. Are you getting to the point in your investing timeline where you need to flex your risk profile down a notch? If so, make the changes and rebalance your portfolio in line with the new allocation.

Next, make sure you **rebalance** the mix of assets back to the starting allocation. This is counter-intuitive as it involves selling things which are doing well and buying things that are not doing so well. But you must do it, because otherwise your portfolio risks getting out of kilter, even to the point of moving into a risk category that you didn't intend.

Finally, having rebalanced the portfolio, you can also look at the performance of the component parts. For each one, consider the following measures over three-year periods:

⇨ **Three-year performance** – should be second quartile or above, that means the fund should be above the sector average.

⇨ **Three-year volatility** – should be below average for its sector. This is one measure of the risk taken by a fund to achieve its aims.

⇨ **Three-year Sharpe ratio** (another measure to help compare the risk taken and returns achieved by each fund) – should be above average for its sector.

⇨ For actively managed components of the portfolio, the **three-year Alpha** (a measure of how much added-value the manager has provided) should be above average for its sector.

Each of the above measures refers to the fund's Investment Association sector. These are groups of similarly constructed funds which allow you to see how your fund compares against its peers. If your chosen fund is consistently above average (or below average for volatility) in its sector, you can be confident that it is doing its job for you as part of your portfolio.

By measuring over three years, you will be assessing the consistency of a fund over time, rather than its less relevant short-term performance.

The easiest way to find this information is to search by sector on the free FE Trustnet website at www.trustnet.co.uk. This will show all the funds in the given sector. To make life easier, you may want to apply some filters to reduce the number of funds in the table, for example, only showing funds with at least three 'crowns' or reducing the FE Risk Score slider to half the available range.

You can then set up a custom table showing the four measures above, and while the sector average won't show up in the table, you can sort the columns in order and work out the average from there.

Rinse and repeat

The vast majority of people reading this will opt for the portfolio fund approach, maybe with some satellite holdings round the side as they get used to the practice of investing.

Investing really is a simple process, and only needs to get as complex and involved as you want it to be.

Spread your money around using an off-the-shelf fund or two, or a portfolio of a few funds you have chosen. Keep the asset allocation and the underlying funds under review once a year to make sure everything's on track.

Staying the Course

IT CAN BE EXCITING GETTING started with your wealth-building efforts. But life is essentially a grind and the long-term nature of investing means it can be easy to lose sight of the reasons you're doing all this in the first place.

Here are some things you should keep in mind as you go through life. These are the secrets to staying on track and rekindling the excitement you felt at the beginning.

1. Auto-increases

The magic of automatic increases to your savings levels cannot be overstated and the difference it will make to the eventual outcome of all your efforts is profound.

Let's say a 30-year-old starts saving £50 per month into a pension, which earns a return of 6% per year.

If she never increases her payment from the £50 per month, when she gets to age 60, she will have a fund worth £50,281.

If she increases her payment by £10 per month each year, when she reaches age 60, her fund will be worth £154,284 – over three times as much.

If she was to increase her payment by 10% per month each year, she would have £186,123 in her fund at age 60.

Such is the power of small, regular increases. These increases will be barely noticeable each year, but over time they make a big difference.

Seeing your fund rise more each year because of the added money you are paying in will keep you excited about the journey.

2. Regular reviews

We talked in the last chapter about reviewing your investment portfolio, but there is much more to financial success than good investing.

Every year you should review your goals, your timescales and your life circumstances to make sure everything is still as it was and that your progress is on track.

Have you received a pay rise? If so, do you need to increase your savings rate? Have your circumstances changed in such a way that you may need to review your life insurance provision? Have you received an inheritance or had a larger than-expected tax bill? What needs to change in light of these new inputs?

Sitting down once a year, or between times if needed, is a good way to revisit your goals and get excited about them again. Being intentional and proactive about your financial life will make you feel in control and means that you don't have to think too much about it between reviews.

3. Get your partner onside

Just as it is easier to budget if both parties to a partnership are onside, it also makes it easier to work towards and stick to your goals if both of you are heading in the same direction.

That doesn't mean that both parties have to be equally involved at all levels of the family finances. We all have our strengths and it is likely that one partner is more suited to the day-to-day management than the other. But when it comes to the big picture stuff, the planning, the dreaming and the strategising, it is best if you are both involved.

Make a date and sit down and talk this through. Do you still want the same things in retirement? Are your timescales the same? Has one partner had enough of their job and would like a career change, perhaps? What difference might this make to your financial planning?

Treat reluctant financial partners gently; don't force them to be more involved than they want to be. If they trust you to handle everything, then great. Don't ever make your partner feel they're being obstructive. Instead, try to get them onside by sharing how excited you are about the family's financial future as you build towards your goals.

4. Be aware of your behavioural biases

As much as I have tried to teach you about how investments work and why you should let markets do their thing to build your wealth over time, you are still human.

This means that you will react emotionally towards your money, when in the perfect world you really shouldn't.

I remember seeing newspaper headlines during the financial crisis of 2008. They screamed ARMAGEDDON and MELTDOWN in huge letters and showed jagged red arrows pointing down and smashing into the ground. It's hard to see that, knowing your pension fund is invested in stock markets, and not get a little concerned.

As you become more experienced, you should be able to shrug off negative news more easily, but you'll always be human. Seeing your portfolio go down in value for two or three years running is hard for anyone to take.

How can you make it easier to stick to your plans, even when everyone else seems to be panicking? Here are some ideas:

⇨ **Don't check your portfolio value too often** – this encourages short-term thinking and when investing you should always think long term.

⇨ **Keep the end in mind** – if you are working towards a goal which is 20 years into the future, remember that current difficulties are most likely a blip along the way.

⇨ **Expend energy on the investing disciplines** – rebalancing, reassessing your timescale and asset allocation, and increasing your savings rate, are all good uses of your mental energy and leave less room for worrying about short-term market events

⇨ **Remember, you can never time the markets** – you might like to think that you can make a positive difference to your portfolio value by doing something, anything, like tweaking the fund choice, or even selling all your investments and holding the money safely in the bank for a while. The reality is that you will be better off leaving things alone. You will never get the timing perfectly right, so why bother?

Staying the course is not easy, but remember no one is going to do this for you. A few simple disciplines repeated over and over again will ensure you reach your goals in great financial shape, but you have to adopt these disciplines. Automate what you can, be intentional about the rest, review things often. Rinse and repeat.

When and How to Use a Financial Adviser

MEANINGFULMONEY WAS SET UP WITH the hope that many more people would be able to take control of their personal finances without the help of a financial adviser. By arming you with just the information you need with minimal jargon, I hope to equip you to set things up correctly and stay the course over the rest of your life.

I remain convinced that most ordinary people don't need financial advice to get started. While everyone can benefit from some quality time with a competent financial planner, not everyone wants to open up to a stranger about their finances, and not everyone is in the position to pay an adviser's fees, especially when starting out.

If building wealth really is about the three steps of spending less than you earn, insuring against disaster, and investing wisely using pensions, ISAs and a diversified portfolio of investments, then anyone can do it. Yes, YOU can do it. I have countless emails from listeners to MeaningfulMoney who have got themselves out of debt and started building wealth on their own, without the help of an adviser.

But there may be times in your financial life when you get overwhelmed with the number of things to think about and take action upon.

There are a few times like that when it really does make sense to seek professional advice:

⇨ When you are considering the prospect of retirement and want to plan how and when you should go about taking benefits from your different pensions and other assets. This is the key point in your financial life when **everyone** should see an adviser.

⇨ If you receive an unexpected lump sum of money from an inheritance or lottery win, and life essentially changes overnight.

⇨ If your partner dies and you need some hand-holding as you come to terms with the financial implications of your loss.

⇨ If you end up acting as a trustee, executor or power of attorney for someone else. In this case you're dealing with other people's money and it can help protect you to have a professional involved.

⇨ If you have complex pension arrangements from years gone by, especially final salary pensions.

How to find a good adviser

1. Ask your friends for a referral

The easiest way to find an adviser is to ask your friends and family if they have dealt with an adviser they trust. It's a start, but shouldn't be the only criteria you use in choosing an adviser.

Facebook has a recommendation feature which can help you cast the net wider.

2. Use sourcing sites

There are websites dedicated to helping members of the public find an adviser by searching around their postcode. Unbiased, VouchedFor and Adviserbook are key players in this space, but others are also available. If you do a search for 'Find a financial adviser in your town' one or more of these adviser search sites will come up.

These sites are free for the public to use, but advisers can pay to have their listings placed higher in the rankings, so bear this in mind.

3. Visit the firm's website

Next, check out the website of any adviser you're considering talking to. Many advisers' websites are pretty vanilla, so if you find one that stands out, that's usually a good thing.

Read the words carefully. They should talk about you more than themselves. They should talk about helping you plan and realising your goals far more than they talk about products like pensions and ISAs. Watch any videos on the site to get a sense of the people involved and the process that the adviser will take you through

Are there testimonials? If so, treat them with a pinch of salt, unless they carry the full names of the people involved.

4. Check the FCA register

You must ensure that any adviser you talk to is regulated by the Financial Conduct Authority and is on the FCA Register. Look for the adviser's Firm Reference Number or FRN on their website, and then go to **register.fca.org.uk**, put in the number and check out the firm's listing.

From there you can click through to the individual adviser working for that firm and see if they have been disciplined by the regulator in the past.

5. Look for chartered or certified status

The minimum standard for a financial adviser in the UK is a financial planning diploma. You can set your sights higher than the minimum standard by looking for a Chartered Financial Planner or a Certified Financial Planner, the latter of these may be shortened to CFP.

These sound very similar, but are very different qualifications. Chartered Financial Planners have to sit a series of high-level exams to attain the qualification, but the assessment of how they can apply their knowledge to practical client situations is limited.

A Certified Financial Planner, on the other hand, as well as having the head knowledge, has been extensively assessed on their ability to apply that knowledge to real-world situations.

If you can find an adviser who has both qualifications, so much the better.

Be aware, though, that a high-level of qualification does not automatically mean they are a good adviser. There are unfortunately still too many highly-qualified crooks and charlatans around.

6. Meet with one or more potential advisers

Almost all advisers will meet with you for a free session to get to know you and your situation, and to see if they can help. This is a courtship – do you like them, do they like you, do you trust each other?

The financial planner/client relationship is a pretty deep one, where you will have to bare your financial soul to a stranger, so you need to get on with them. Trust your gut here. Your first instinct about an adviser is likely the right one.

Don't be in a rush to sign up with the first adviser you meet. If they're any good, they'll give you all the time you need to come to a decision.

Ask any potential adviser how they get paid. All advisers dealing with pensions and investments have to work on a fee basis now, as commission was abolished back in 2013.

Be wary of any adviser who only gets paid when you agree to sign up to a product through them. The best advisers will charge you for advice whether or not you take it up – that's the fairer way to do it because that way, you know their advice is not leading you towards a product just so the adviser can get paid.

If you think the adviser is charging you too much, tell them, and ask them to justify why their fees are at that level. If you're not convinced there's value in the process for you, walk away.

7. Ask your adviser to commit to a service standard

The financial planning process can be broken down into three stages:

1. **Planning** – where the adviser will collate a clear picture of your current financial position, work with you to establish your goals and come up with a plan to help you reach them.

2. **Implementation** – where the necessary products are arranged to help you achieve your goals, or where things like wills, trusts, and fund switches are put in place to set you on the right track.

3. **Review** – a regular meeting where the adviser will discuss the performance of your portfolio, but more importantly catch up with you and your life circumstances to see if any changes are needed to the financial plan.

Too many advisers promise to review your circumstances regularly, but end up not doing so. Make sure your adviser has a process to review your situation to help keep you on track.

8. Hold your adviser to account

Once you have committed to working with an adviser over a period of time, make sure they are honouring the service promises they made at the outset. Always remember that you are paying fees to your adviser and that money could be in your pocket if you opted for a do-it-yourself approach.

An adviser will add value in some tangible ways and some less tangible ones. If they rebalance your portfolio and work to reduce the costs of your holdings by switching funds and providers, then that's clear – they have added value by reducing your costs.

If they make your portfolio more tax-efficient by helping you use the various allowances, that's a clear and tangible benefit too.

But they may also be a sounding board when you are worried about markets and help you to stay invested when you're thinking about bailing out. When markets come back into positive territory, you may not be able to put a number on what the adviser saved you by helping you to stay invested, but it will be significant. And the peace of mind you can gain by having a trusted adviser managing your financial plan with you is very difficult to quantify.

You will know, deep down, if the adviser relationship you have is a healthy one or not. If not, don't be afraid to go it alone or work with someone else. Your chosen adviser must earn their keep. If they don't, it isn't a healthy relationship, and you need to end it.

Over to You

IF YOU'VE MADE IT THIS far, you are now equipped with everything you need to KNOW and everything you need to DO to secure your financial future.

Remember the three steps:

1. Spend less than you earn.
2. Insure against disaster.
3. Invest wisely.

Continuing to walk these three steps consistently over a lifetime guarantees financial success. You can now take all you have learned and begin to apply it.

Remember, you don't have to do everything at once. First master the discipline of spending less than you earn, and then, once any bad debt is cleared, use that regular money-saving discipline to start investing.

One final point. Very few, if any, of the decisions you make regarding your finances will be irreversible, so if you make a mistake, you can pivot and set off on a different path. By being intentional about your finances and reviewing things regularly, you will quickly spot if things are not as they should be.

This should free you from over-agonising about any one decision. Instead, make a choice and execute. Then, on review, you can see if the decision you took was the right one.

Remember that there are many more resources over at the MeaningfulMoney website. There are hundreds of podcast episodes and videos, as well as a couple of courses and eBooks to help you with your budgeting and investing.

I sincerely hope that this book has helped clarify some of the seemingly impenetrable terms and phrases we love to use in financial services. And I hope it has inspired you to take control of your own finances.

I know that if you follow the three steps consistently over time, you will secure your financial future. And I'd love to hear from you about the progress you're making. So get in touch via the website and let's talk.

I wish you the very best of luck.